I0757043

Move On

Refuse to Stay Stuck

WALTER BOSTON, JR.

authorHOUSE

AuthorHouse™
1663 Liberty Drive
Bloomington, IN 47403
www.authorhouse.com
Phone: 1 (800) 839-8640

Cover Design
Eric Harris
eharris04@gmail.com

Photo taken by
Walter Boston, III
walterboston3@gmail.com

Edited by
Anita R. Thompson
ar_thomp_ca@yahoo.com

Photo edited by
Lisa Wright
lisawrightdance@yahoo.com

Photo advisor
James "Maceo" Harris
godstyles@gmail.com

Published by AuthorHouse   05/03/2019

ISBN: 978-1-7283-1016-9 (sc)
ISBN: 978-1-7283-1018-3 (hc)
ISBN: 978-1-7283-1017-6 (e)

Library of Congress Control Number: 2019942833

*This is a personal development, leadership resource written and
distributed for all audiences worldwide!*

Print information available on the last page.

Contents

Randy Boyd, Executive Director, Prepare International and author of

Heaven's Culture

Lubbock, Texas

Dr. Boston does more than move your heart, he leads you on a journey from where you are to where you're supposed to be!

Richard L. Hilton, Founding Pastor

Calvary Church

Johnson City, Tennessee

Words of wisdom concerning a state we have all experienced at one time or another. Call it being in a rut, hitting the wall, plateauing, etc. we have all encountered the situation of being "stuck". Though pursued through the perspective of biblical principles in many cases, the wisdom Dr. Boston imparts in this book is applicable to people of all walks of life. I am confident his practical advice, when applied, can help us all - "Move On".

Tom Kipp, Business Leader/President

Kernersville, North Carolina

Wow!!! So true, so clear, so profound, ...and so practical, sobering and challenging.

"Being stuck is one thing as we all have been in that spot and at times, you have no choice but for a season. Staying stuck is another thing, no one has to stay stuck — not even you!"

"The reality is if something is not moving it is standing still; if it is standing still it is not changing and; if it is not changing it is dying."

Those two quotes are perfect overview of the whole content of this great book.

I believe that everyone reading it may find himself at least in one of two situations: in a need to get out of stuck or to learn how to avoid one.

Thank you dear Walter for such a useful tool.

Wieslaw Ziemba, Poland

European Church and Marketplace Leader

You hold in your hands a priceless resource that will absolutely empower you to move beyond the rut you may be in.

Dr. Boston has taken a complex subject — the reasons and ways we become stuck in life — and created an easy to read self-help manual. Amazing! I am devouring this book! I refuse to be stuck any longer!

Barbara Brown, Pastor

River of Life Worship Center

Odenton, Maryland

On this journey of life we all inevitably reach a level where we feel stuck. This feeling of being stuck impacts us holistically, spiritually and mentally. Dr Boston in his humorous and honest way offers us nuggets of wisdom that are practical and very much in touch with reality. This book simplifies and contextualizes the struggle and ushers us into a season where we can "MOVE ON".

Brandon Bailey, Lead Pastor,

Teleios Church

Johannesburg, South Africa

Do you find your life is in a rut despite all your efforts to break free? The frustration can be unbearable at times. How do we overcome pain, difficulty and failure? Has progress in your life come to a halt? Here is a book that will not only provide you with practical solutions to these and other heart wrenching issues but walk you through them step by step.

Dr. Boston brings his life long experience of more than four decades of working with individuals, church and corporate leadership globally. Every chapter is packed with life-giving nuggets to get you moving again. Understand the debilitating power of attraction, addiction and affection and how to be free. Learn how to make good friends and how to stop self-hurt and self-harm, appreciate the value of confronting your feelings, the components of Dr. Boston's "Destructive Behavioral Syndromes" (DBS) and much more.

As you read, you will experience a life coach coming alongside you to help you *Move On*. It is backed up with real-life stories of people, like a young mother who cooked her baby alive in an oven, and to see how some broke free and Moved On!

This is a must read for all leaders and individuals alike who are determined to *MOVE ON and refuse to be stuck.*

Trevor Joefield

President, Ministers Fellowship West Indies

Trinidad, West Indies

Dr. Walter Boston, Jr. with his jovial personality and his easy to read compilation of an amazing book, "*MOVE ON – Refuse to Stay Stuck*" will be the external force to propel you to new realms in your walk with the Lord!

And it could also provide the new, critical thinking that is needed to solve many of the problems facing so many in the world and in the Church today!

The nuggets of truth contained within the pages of this book will certainly encourage and also equip you to be all that the Father has ordained for you to become.

Read, enjoy and then *MOVE ON!*

Walter, thank you for over 25 years of friendship and leadership!

Michael Scantlebury – Apostle

Dominion-Life International Ministries

Author of, *As It Was In the Beginning… So Shall It Be*

Surrey, Canada

Acknowledgments

I continue to be overwhelmed by the exemplary people in my life. Every time I reminisce, I vividly see a host of super, amazing, gifted, loving, selfless and extremely competent people who simply make me look better than I am.

My name is on the front of the book as the author; but, I have argued over and over that it shouldn't be — and I mean it. And only this one time, I am right!

So, to my Lord Jesus Christ, who gives me wisdom to write; my family who stands by this dreamer-boy; my proof-reader/editor who helps me to clearly convey what I have attempted to write; my graphic designer who captures my words in pictures and images; my photographer who make this boy look like Hollywood brass; my publisher who has done it for me a third time now; my financier who paid for this entire project (I could not have it without him); my partners and followers who buy this book as without them there would be no one to share my gift of leadership with; my friends who tell me, "Walter, write, folks will read your stuff;" my intercessors who pray for me day in and day out (because of them, I am still going)…

Ok, just er'body, who did anything to make this possible — THANK YOU!

You should know...

When I first wrote the acknowledgments it was a mini-chapter that looked like a few chapters out of Chronicles in the Bible. Names where everywhere for a couple pages on! So I had to scrap it because I feared I'd left someone out unintentionally and I'd never want to commit such an oversight in crime. So, now as you read this single page you will see categories. You know where you fit. There I am naming you —put on your ultra-ray cool shades or glasses to see it — and applauding for you for a job well done!

Sincerely, I thank you for writing this book, giving it to the world and allowing me to put my name on the front as the author.

You are way too kind... and I LOVE YOU ALL!

Dedication

This book is dedicated to YOU! You hold in your hands a resource that I trust you will consult time and time again when you get stuck for whatever reason. May something in the book always be a relevant solution to empower you to MOVE ON! I dedicate this to your forward movement and personal happiness and fulfillment!

Foreword

By: Jack R. Taylor

This is a remarkable book by a remarkable man and my spiritual son, Walter Boston, Jr. I clearly remember the day when he drove a good distance to ask me the question about becoming a spiritual son. That day began a treasured relationship between me and one of the most powerful thinkers I have ever known.

When I opened the manuscript and read the title, I wondered what he would do with the word "stuck" and was impressed with the suggestion to "MOVE ON". I should have known to expect something like what happened, but suddenly I realized that I was the counselee and the author was my counselor. I shall never be the same!

There is not one among us who has not experienced being stuck, stopped, stymied and stilled. So the event of being stuck is common and quite understandable but when "stuck" becomes a condition, many of our productive mechanisms for progress and success grind to a halt. I was avid and attentive for the unplanned hours it took to go

through this very valuable book. The result? I am a wiser
and better man for having spent this time studying "stuck"
and am more determined than ever to "MOVE ON"!

Thanks, Walter Son, for this small book with a very huge
and hopefully heeded suggestion to us all to "MOVE ON"!

Jack Taylor, President
Dimensions Ministries
Melborne, Florida

Introduction

MOVE ON - Refuse to Stay Stuck

It takes little to no effort to get in a rut. Just don't do anything and you will stay in the same place — I guarantee it.

Iyanla Vanzant, a popular American inspirational speaker says, *"When you have something to do life will not allow you to move forward until you do it." "Doing it"* is the big challenge right? This is especially true if your life seems to be working just fine. Why move on? Move on to what? Move on to where? Move on how? These are just a few thoughts we all entertain. Frankly, it is easier to keep things the same as they are than to do something new, something different. It is less hassle, headache, and heartache. And after all, if your life is working there is no rut. So what is the issue? And oh yeah, you are very good at the rut you have been in for the past years, really good at it! Practice makes perfect, right?

Really?

Are you sure about the "life working just fine" thing? If everything is so fine then why do you keep having battles within your heart and mind about where you are? Do you keep humming the song, "Is That All There is?" The uneasiness keeps getting more and more uneasy and it is bothering the heck out of you. Why did the title of this book capture your interest so quickly and boldly? Is it really working just fine?

Hmmm… you are stuck and you know it. Pardon my straightforwardness, but I want to help you. I do not say this to hurt you. Nor do I want you to quit your job, abandon your responsibilities, join a band of gypsies travelling through and the next thing you know, you are wearing a kerchief, colorful clothes, and you have changed your name to Zoltan. Being stuck leaves you in "frozen" mode. You don't feel as though you are accomplishing much in your life despite the fact that you take care of your family and are a star at your job, but there is something deep within that resonates and questions inwardly with driving force asking, "Is this all there is?" You are neither cool nor comfortable with being stuck, and I am here to say that neither should you be comfortable in that position. You are simply just putting up with it. Just maybe you have put up with it long enough! I just want to help you.

To add to your misery, everybody else knows you are stuck and it is becoming an embarrassing and nearly unbearable situation. It is hurting how you function in life. You are starting to feel a bit upset and maybe even angry about the rut. Ok. It is driving you nuts!

Several years ago, I was out with an acquaintance and we were doing lunch. I had been providing spiritual and professional coaching and we were using the lunch to ratify our discussions. As we arrived at the restaurant and got out of the vehicle, unknowingly to me, he had gotten stuck between the seat and the door of the car. When I looked back and realized he was stuck I broke out into laughter. It was so hilarious — I kid you not! My automatic reaction was laughter as it appeared to be as simple as opening up a car door. And if you know me, you KNOW that I find humor in the simplest of things — laughing is medicine for the heart and soul. The funny part wasn't that he was stuck, but rather the hilarious body motions and facial expression he was making were causing me to laugh myself silly and to weep a deluge of tears. I could not stop laughing. I am pretty sure my laughter was upsetting to him as the frustration on his part did nothing to release him from his prison of "stuck-ness." I looked back and saw him twisting and turning and moving back and forth, but oddly, he could not move forward or backwards no matter how hard he tried. I asked him what was wrong. He replied, *"I am stuck. My shoestring is caught under the car seat."* And then, I only started to laugh more because by this time the pitch of his voice had gone from mid-range tenor to high soprano. He wasn't in shock, but he was very embarrassed that he was stuck — and understandably so. I saw him moving back and forth and he was able to turn a bit, but, he could not move forward. Now get the image of a roughly 5'9" (or 175 cm) man with a medium build stuck in a rut in the driver's seat in a car he had control of. The car door was there, but in the position he was caught, he could only twist and turn but go nowhere in the attempt to free himself. Now you are laughing — stop it! He was moving, but not from that place because he was stuck. He was just moving around and about in the same place.

I tried to get myself together. I tried to suppress my laughter so I could go over to help the brother out. He had been relentlessly fighting for his physical freedom for nearly a minute — way too long! Even as I type this, I am laughing because I see it playing out in my mind all over again.

As I cautiously moved in closer to speak to him in a low voice so that nobody would be privy to our conversation, and to ensure that he would not whack me upside my head, I asked, "Why are you doing this?" He said in a mildly harsh tone, *"I am trying to get unstuck but the string won't untangle from underneath the car seat. I didn't get myself stuck it just happened!"* I then replied, "I see that you are stuck, but why don't you just pull the shoe off and untangle it from the bottom of the car seat? If you will do that you can stop moving around in the same place and we can move forward. Dude, right now you are making me laugh. And other folks are starting to look over and they are laughing too. You have been moving back and forth making these hilarious motions for almost a minute. Just take your shoe off, Sir!"

It was then that he had a heavenly awakening. He realized that his being stuck had clouded his ability to make a simple but rational decision to remove the shoe so he could untangle the culprit and then move forward. On the way into the restaurant, he suddenly broke out laughing. Yeah, it registered, and in the aftermath, he thought it was the funniest thing ever!

My acquaintance's actions that unforgettable summer day are so indicative of many people and the way they act today. They are moving for all intents and purposes, but stay in the same place because they are stuck. While stuck in the same place they are expending a lot of energy while drawing unnecessary attention to themselves. All they need to do is to remove the shoe, then the string from the bottom of the seat will give way, the shoe can then be put back on, and the captive is then free to move on. Simple as simple can be, but not always obvious in the moment.

Listen, you have this book in your hands right at this moment for a reason and it is not coincidental. I want you to seriously consider what type of rut you are in and how it is keeping you from moving on. Deep down within you recognize that you need to move on, but you are stuck.

Take a serious and honest look around you — outside of your small private world — have you moved lately, I mean really moved on? Could you sadly boast and even get the "decade award" for faithfully maintaining the same place in life, going through the same motions everyday — moving, but not going anywhere? Nothing has changed in years and furthermore, you are clueless as to how to move because your brain is clouded and your body chained by the rut you are in.

There are many ways and reasons why we get stuck. Not all reasons are as simple as the shoestring and car seat analogy. We all have our unique stories of getting stuck in ruts — some simple and some severe. Do you have a testimony or two or three or four? If you don't, I personally have at least a million personal moments I can share with you. Ok, maybe not a million but at least nine hundred and ninety-nine thousand!

So let me ask you a few questions.

If you could move on from a rut would you?

Have you been in your rut so long that you prefer not to be bothered?

Would you prefer to just leave things quietly and comfortably as they are?

Have you had enough of the rut and you want to pull the shoe off, untangle yourself and move on?

Whether you are stuck and know it or stuck and do not know it, I can assure you, you do not want to be stuck. When you are stuck you can still move, but it doesn't mean you are going forward. In fact, you are likely just moving around in the same place and there can be nothing productive or fruitful about moving around in the same place. The only reason anyone would stay in a rut in the same place, is because they have a defeating love with the "same ole, same ole" and an aversion to any kind of change. I have to be the one to tell you that this would make you by definition a nut. And frankly, that is not cool!

So, may I propose to you that we explore how to become unstuck and move on?

Before we go any further in the book, I will be very forthcoming with you and am telling you up-front that it will help if you make a firm decision this very moment to refuse to be stuck. Reading the book for results requires that you make a resolute decision — a refusal to be stuck.

Being stuck is one thing as we all have been in that spot and at times, you have no choice but for a season. Once that season passes, staying stuck is another thing, no one has to stay stuck — not even you!

ONE
How Did I Get Stuck

A few years ago, I was traveling across Kenya to serve several hundred leaders and their churches. I had already completed my assignment in five of the coastal cities including Mombasa and a few places near the Tanzanian border. I will not name the Border cities as it is primarily Muslim territory and I could put the Christian leaders who serve there in harm's way. It was an intriguing journey including a ride on a huge ferryboat that transported us to the Border port towns. I taught twenty-three times in five days and the end of my assignment was nowhere in sight. Despite the fast and unyielding pace, I was enjoying every second of meeting, teaching, and interacting with those precious Kenyan leaders.

After many well-spent days in the coastal region of Kenya, I boarded a plane back to Nairobi, where I had entered the country the week before. I was warmly greeted and driven by car into the northern region of Tigoni, Kenya. My host and friends welcomed me to their beautiful home overlooking the city below. This small mountainous area became my home base. I was ready for some much needed

R&R. The next two days, I did just that — rested and relaxed!

We began our week-long teaching journey by vehicle where we would travel for a few hours to a town or village, teach the villagers, layover for the night and then travel to the next one the next morning. Sometimes we would travel by night to the next town. This went on for the next six days. Some of the venues we were booked to teach at were in very remote and hard to get to places. You had to come off the main roads and travel the back roads into the bush. These roads were not paved and were more like foot paths, full of potholes and very narrow. Those conditions alone made for a rough ride, but in addition to it, we had muddy wet surfaces that contained water-filled potholes. In fact, for a few days we traveled in the rain— not light rain by any means, but rather, driving, torrential rains.

As we prepared for our next stop, my host and our driver, had an idea that we should take a different path to what our navigation device was telling us to take. An entire team was traveling in the vehicle which included two of the main leaders of the denomination I was serving and my translator. One of the leaders was familiar with the alternate route that was being suggested and they all agreed that it would be shorter and that we should take it. They felt it would allow us to reach our next destination before night fall.

In a matter of minutes, we were off of the main road and traveling on a wet, narrow road strewn with potholes.

In my estimation it was not a back road at all, but rather a walking path. Nonetheless, it was driven on by the natives with their cars and we passed a car every now and then… and I mean, every now and then. In fact, I saw more people on foot leading their mules hitched to wagons rather than cars. Along the way, I also noticed cars in the ravine — ok, the ditch! The cars slid off the road and had been abandoned by their drivers. The path was in such a dilapidated condition that you could only move about five to ten miles per hour (10 to 15 kilometers) while trying to avoid potholes. Ten miles per hour was speeding on this road. It was like riding a bucking bronco, but worse. We bumped up and down all the way! A person prone to motion sickness would have been in a chronic situation.

All I could think of in my mind was, Lord, please don't let us end up in a ditch! Soon the night would fall and from the looks of things we would be on this path for a long while. I knew in my "knower" that it was not safe to get stuck along this path to seemingly nowhere at night. The natives knew it also. It wasn't all that safe driving through there in the daylight hours, let alone through the dark of night. The possibility of being robbed or worse was likely. Just as I was thinking and praying inwardly not to get stuck — you guessed it — the truck spun off the path and into the ravine. I wondered to myself whether my thinking about us winding up in the ditch got us into this messy situation. The driver spoke up and said, "No problem guys, this is a four wheel drive and we should be able to get out with no problem at all." He gave a few instructions, we followed them and he proceeded to try and get the truck out of the ravine. But, it was not happening. The truck was spinning and it was going nowhere. We were stuck!

For the next few moments the host and leaders onboard used every trick in the book to get us out — nothing was working. They even had me out there alongside them pushing the truck. Let me tell you, that was an Instagram, Twitter or Facebook moment for sure. It would have gotten a lot of likes and possibly would have gone viral because it was hilarious! I had my boots on — not working boots either — and I was slowly losing traction while trying to push that doggone truck out of the ravine. They had to catch me a time or two to keep me from sliding or falling into the mud. Listen, it was one of those moments where it was very serious and very funny at the same time. Even now as I reflect back on it I am laughing. I wasn't laughing that day — none of us were. I was scared out of my wits!

After an extended time of trying to get the truck unstuck, the leaders said, "The guys over across the path can get us out, but we will have to pay them. They get people out all the time. They know the exact angle to position and push the truck and they will have us out in minutes. In fact, they have been watching us the entire time. They are just waiting for us to call them over so they can make some money. They will not volunteer to come, but they will help if we offer shillings." Kenyan Shillings is the currency used in Kenya. This is when the female host started to grin — more of a smirk than a grin, but nonetheless a grin as she knew all along what would have been the most effective way to get us unstuck, but she kept her peace and said nothing. Women have a wonderful gift called intuition, and men fail time and time again by not recognizing that gift and what it might be saying about a certain situation.

So finally it was mutually agreed upon that we should call them over to help us. And it happened just as the leaders said it would. In fact, in less than a minute we were unstuck. They were paid and off we went bumping down the path again. For a moment in time, it felt like that I was praying to everybody out in the stratosphere asking for help. I did not want to stay stuck and I did not want to get stuck again. And oh yeah, just in case the Lord was busy, I thought for just a brief second I might give the other alleged religious deities a chance! I am just kidding here! I was one grateful fella that the Lord had come to our rescue through those village gentlemen. Frankly, I was ready to give them all the shillings I had on me.

How did we get stuck anyway?

Before the accident we were moving along just fine and the driver had the driving all under control. We felt safe and secure. He was a really good driver and knew how to navigate the Kenyan roads and paths. He had done very well so far and we'd already covered hundreds of miles or kilometers. We were also traveling in a four wheel drive SUV that was suited for this sort of terrain. It appeared that the odds of us getting stuck were minimal. The regular two wheel drive cars, yes, they would likely get stuck, but us in our four wheel drive, we arrogantly assumed within ourselves that you just don't get stuck with a four wheel drive, definitely not! But even with that smug assurance, here we were stuck big-time and I mean stuck! So much for assumptions, huh?

This incident mirrors our lives on many levels. Over many years, I have noticed several ways that we get stuck in life and many of them appear to be similar to the trip on that fateful day in Kenya along the water-filled potholed road.

We are always in a state of change whether we realize it or not and we all need to change, all of the time. We go from being dependent children in our parents' care to independent single people earning a living at our first job after college, possibly marrying and raising a family and then the season shifts to the empty nest or the welcoming of grandchildren. Whether you are a person of faith or not, life is never in a state of standing still. It is in a state of full on flux. We must change and most of it is progressive and for our good.

For the Christian, his or her journey is meant to be one of change where the believer is continually being transformed into the image and likeness of God's Son, Jesus Christ. This happens in various stages, and from the beginning of putting our faith in Jesus Christ, it is a logical progression of growth. No matter what season of life we are in, God intends for us to grow and mature. So how does that change come about in our lives and what role do you as a believer play in the process of change? In the first place, how do we get stuck?

It is so very human to avoid change as the adage of "if it ain't broke, don't fix it" becomes the fabric of our everyday lives and relationships. We will avoid pain at all costs in the moment until the situation becomes so painful and we cannot stand it anymore, then we think maybe it is time to change. You have to approach the desire to change with a gutsy attitude and a mandate of personal prayer that says to the Lord, "Lord, help me to feel enough pain to make me desire change, not just the appearance of change, but change at my very core."

So we have ascertained that we need to change, but first we will look at four ways we can get stuck. These are not exhaustive, but they are in my estimation the most common and initial ways we get stuck in life. There are plenty of other ways and I'm sure you could add a few of your own unique experiences to this chapter.

First, you can get stuck by accident. By this I mean your situation was not intentional. You were simply taking the ride of life when suddenly the unexpected happened and you cannot move forward or backwards. You are moving, but, you are not making traction and thus not moving forward. Our incident that day was purely an accident. The truck hit a deep pothole filled with water which caused us to mildly hydroplane into the ravine. We were dwellers in a ditch before we knew it. The driver did not hit the pothole intentionally. He was doing an outstanding job of avoiding them, but it happened anyway. It was really an accident.

It has happened to you too hasn't it?

You were moving along just fine, hit a pothole in life, and could not get out. When you tried, you realized you were stuck — moving but going nowhere, running on the spot as it were, spinning your tires and making the ruts deeper. The initial thought was, "How did this happen?" You were doing everything just right and it happened anyway. At times like this, the human reaction is usually to accept the lot in life for what it is, and when you are stricken with that mindset and you do not look beyond the situation to change it, nor purpose in your mind to only settle for a time, it quickly becomes a lifelong existence. Beware of settling in any spot for very long as it can strip you of a vibrant, fulfilling life.

When you get stuck because of an accident, the best thing to do is to call for help. I once had a seasoned administrative assistant who would say in our team meetings, *"If you don't know what you are doing you'd better ask somebody!"* Her advice was very apropos in that day and continues to be so. And it probably applies to your life today if you are stuck. Don't ever assume that trying to get unstuck on your own is the high road. You'll just dredge deeper and deeper into your rut. Call out, call loudly or scream if you have to!

I am confident we could have saved some precious minutes that day if we would have asked for help after two failed attempts. Some of us would have stayed warm and dry rather than becoming mud-soaked zombie-like creatures.

However, the truck was filled with guys and just one lady. Need I say any more on that one? We were beyond two failed attempts and still trying to get out. The sweet lady who was our host, had suggested after our first two failed attempts that we ask the guys across the path to help. But, we had it under control — you know, the guys had it all taken care of — right! And like guys do, after it became our idea and not our sweet lady's idea, we asked the roadside crew standing by with expected payment to help get us out.

There is nothing to be embarrassed about if you are stuck because of an accident — a situation that has happened beyond your control. While the situation itself may be embarrassing, you don't need to be embarrassed or ashamed. Author, Sandeep Jauhar says, *"The only mistake you can make is not asking for help."* I think this is especially true when you are stuck and you have been stuck for an extended period of time.

Getting stuck is common in life. It is more common than we all care to admit. An honest look back over our lives will attest that it is commonplace. Things happen. Things that we did not plan. No one plans to be stuck. However, when it happens we should call out for help. I strongly caution not to be among the many who choose not to call for help because it can be to your detriment. In chapter four we will discuss what kind of help you should look for. I cannot wait to discuss the types of help you should seek out in those times with you in detail.

If you have had an accident and it has left you stuck in something, someone is waiting to help you get unstuck. They may just be watching you spin in the same place waiting for you to call out for "Help!" The moment you do, they will know exactly what to do to get you out of the ditch! You may have to pay a little cash, or wash the mud off your face, but it will be worth it to get unstuck.

Second, you can get stuck by being inattentive. There are times when we make the mistake of not heeding the warning signs that are blaring right in our faces! The sad thing about this type of entrapment is that we see it and are very aware of it, but we just carelessly neglect what we see. How many times have you been stuck and you said, "I knew that was going to happen. I saw it coming." However you continued on anyway towards the torpedo coming your way. Perhaps the thrill of the dalliance with the entrapment was what veered you off the safe path. It happens time and time again.

When we turned on the dirt road that day, I knew that we were bound for trouble. It was inevitable. There was even a suggestion made that we should turn around and get back on the main road because just a few seconds in on the secondary road, we were sliding and bumping all over the place. Besides this, the path was going to be several kilometers or miles of travel before we saw the main road again. We did not pay attention to what the dirt road was telling us. It was telling us, screaming at us, "I will not let you pass without a challenge. And, I will likely win the challenge." And it did.

Think of a few incidents in your life when you got stuck. You are having an "aha" moment right now aren't you? After being in the situation for a while you probably castigated yourself with phrases like: "I should have paid attention, or why did I allow myself to let this happen? I should not have neglected my inner voice that was screaming in my head, don't go there!"

Neglecting warning signs is never wise and especially when they are clear warning signs. The best thing you can do is to stop and consider why you are being warned. King Solomon, one of the writers of the book of Proverbs has something to say about this. He says, *"Wisdom shouts in the streets. She cries out"* Proverbs 1:20. When something is shouting at you, stop and listen. Don't neglect it. Even if you feel you have got it all under control, stop and listen to the other side of reasoning that is shouting at you. Especially when it is shouting in the streets… or from a dirt path or when you are in a ravine with rain pouring down on you.

We were in a four-wheel drive truck. Our driver was experienced, but in a later conversation about the incident, we all agreed that just moments after getting on that road we were all thinking we should have turned around. We all made the same mistake and did not speak up even though we were all feeling the same way — with the exception of the lady on board.

If you are stuck in a situation at the moment I suggest you go back and look closely at the details that came to your attention before you first ignored them. You will most likely see some answers on how you got stuck in the first place. Also, there will be answers on how to get unstuck. This action will require you to honestly admit that somewhere you didn't pay attention. Some of us have not paid attention to our "gut" feelings about certain things, places or people. I have known countless people who have said "if I had only listened to my gut." That sense is a God given human radio frequency. Some of us have never trusted our own intuitive ways perhaps due to the fear of being ridiculed. Maybe you were told to "not be so stupid" as a youngster when you shared your thoughts on a situation at hand, and even though you turned out to be right, your parents never gave you credit for your intuitive bent, which caused you to shut down any intuition you might have or thought you had. Parents often fail when navigating child rearing, but intuition is an integral part of the human psyche and regardless of a lack of parental affirmation, it lives on and can be accessed even when it has been suppressed. Please, learn to trust that foreboding in the deep pit of your stomach. It will save you much grief in the future. The foreboding is not there within you due to having had too many spicy chili peppers. It is the God-given intuitive nature shouting the warning that you should heed. You can avoid veering off the path if you do.

I have personally and professionally observed that when you do not pay attention, attention will make you pay. Most of the time it will pay you something you don't want to be paid. I have lead a variety of teams over my four decades of full-time leadership. One principle that I have insistently and consistently taught is: if you don't pay attention to details you can easily derail. I am not upholding that you will automatically derail and I do not want this for you, me or anyone. But, I must forewarn that your chances of derailing are probable. People who pay attention to details are good listeners and good leaders. The end results are that they are good followers. Being a good follower is crucial when you are being warned on any level.

Third, you get stuck when you build friendship with the wrong company. You have probably learned firsthand that friendship with the wrong people can cause things to go wrong really fast. Before you know it, you are stuck in something that is causing personal harm and much more. I am not implying that we can blame other people for our actions. You and I are ultimately responsible for our behavior whether good or bad and we must take responsibility for the choices we make.

Paul the Apostle gives us really straightforward advice on this matter of wrong company. He says, *"Do not be fooled, bad company corrupts good character."* I Corinthians 15:33. Whoa, he doesn't mince his words does he?

He calls certain people "bad company!" He says we are not to fool ourselves into thinking we can have close friendship with them and not have our morals compromised. When our morals are compromised there goes our good character. Hollywood and culture glorifies friendships with bad company and there is something exciting about the gangster films and some of the darker things they portray. The gangster flicks, the molls who rode along with them, the money, the lifestyle, the fancy suits, etc., it is all very attractive on celluloid and in make-believe in one's mind but amusement is just that, it is a panacea of things that just happen in a mode of entertainment that does not mimic real life. Seldom do you see the end results of the gangster having his life taken, or serving a prison sentence that never lets him out on the street again. And to think we sometimes find these films thrilling and we even envy that dangerous lifestyle which plays out on film without consequences. But the reality is, bad company does not take you to the top. In fact, it usually takes you to the bottom when you are hung up, strung out, serving life sentences, hurting and harming people in your path. Sin takes you places that you would not have entered into your GPS as destinations.

I have counseled far too many people — dear and near — who ended up stuck in life because they were fooling around with the wrong people. Frankly, it has happened to me and you as well. No one is proud of the setbacks incurred from our poor relationship choices. This is why our God-given ability to discern must be ready and aimed when building relationships

Compromising relationships will cost you greatly and here are some of the areas affected:

Time that you cannot redeem. There is no such thing as getting missed time back. Once it is gone, it is gone. We only have a small window of time in life — not nearly enough to be stuck in bad behaviors or defeating habits that can be very difficult to overcome. It hurts when any of us get trapped in the abuse and misuse of drugs, alcohol, sex and bad finances to name a few. Many times it takes years to get unstuck from these defeating traps and even if you succeed in getting unstuck, there are whirlpools of repercussion which continue to swirl and haunt you for a long time.

Or perhaps embarrassing legal problems… surely it has gone too far when you end up in a legal situation such as court, jail, or worse because of bad company. Sometimes depending on the offense, you can end up with a negative record that can take years to expunge. You might have to live with that record for the rest of your life which is a huge price to pay for the path of folly.

The most concerning factor is when bad company erodes your character. Character is everything because it is who you are. Who you are will always go with you everywhere you go. You can't leave home without it. No matter what reputation you try to portray, your character will shine brighter. It will shine even when you are trying to hide it.

"Character is like a tree and reputation like a shadow. The shadow is what we think of it' the tree is the real thing." Abraham Lincoln

Fourth, you get stuck when you do not change. The changes we desire in life first start within us with attitudes and mindsets. Without the internal change, our conduct and character will not reflect the change. Once we've recognized our need for change, faith needs to be applied.

When you refuse to change your thinking and behavior you will get stuck in life. Change is the portal to forward movement. When you do not change, you persist in the same old things over and over; you will become irrelevant and end up lagging behind. Ultimately you will be left behind in life. I see this more than I care to admit. I see it in relationships of all kinds: in churches, businesses, communities and even entire regions. I have visited my share of cities and towns and even a few nations that are stuck because they refuse to change. I have visited churches and businesses that I cannot visit anymore because they do not exist anymore. They refused to change and they became irrelevant.

To get stuck in time, old habits and bad traditions is not healthy or honorable. I frequently meet people who want to debate why they are in the sad and despicable place they are in. They argue, "I have been true to my mission and convictions." To this, I respectfully reply, "You have been true to your methods, your old methods that are no longer useful. You have allowed your convictions to become bad traditions that are no longer working. You are stuck."

Heraclitus, the philosopher from Ephesus says, *"Change is constant".*

You and I know this to be true. It is one of the many reasons we do not like change because it happens too frequently and too fast. The moment we get comfortable with the good old way, change makes its rude demands.

Change is also difficult. Here are a few reasons why:

It presents us with the unfamiliar and the unknown.

It rarely comes with understandable or prepackaged instructions.

It causes major inconveniences in what is already working.

It stirs up the fear of the unknown and the fear of failure.

Should I go on? I think you see why it is difficult.

Finally, change is frustrating. It rattles emotions of upset and sometimes even anger within us. It frustrates us when we have to change something that we have already mastered.

All of this said, the bottom line is that if you and I don't want to get stuck in life, in our meaningful relationships, our career and even in our spiritual and personal development, we must change. Gail Sheehy, American author, journalist, and lecturer says, *"If we don't change, we don't grow. If we don't grow, we aren't really living."*

Let me introduce you to five steps to change that I have taught over the years. These are very practical ways that will keep you from getting stuck.

First, you must decide in favor of change. You must resolutely make up your mind that you don't want to stay in the same place you are in now. Every decision in life begins with needing to make our minds up about what we will and will not do. If you cannot make up your mind, you will not move forward. You will be stuck on "stuck."

Second, you must define. You must be clear about what needs to change. You have to be very specific. Generalizations are not enough. If you need to work on some things, what are they? Define them. Write them out and put them where you will be reminded what has to change. Make it a priority.

Third, you must denounce the lack of change. Openly declare that you will not allow the old patterns that you have come to love to remain. These have caused you to remain stuck in your life. With heart determination and courage openly make it formal that you are moving forward. Tell everybody if you have to. Write a personal contract to yourself and sign it. Do whatever it takes!

Fourth, you must declare it loudly and audibly. I have found that when you are trying to move on, it helps to share this news with someone who can cheer you on and hold you accountable as well. We already mentioned it is not easy to change. Therefore, accountability to someone will help you to get unstuck and stay unstuck. A young influential leader in Romania met with me recently and shared that he was stuck when I visited his nation two years prior. After a conversation with me during that visit, I advised him to get an accountability partner. He told me on a recent visit, that he followed my advice and no longer battles with the issue that he confided to me years before.

Fifth, you must defend. By this I mean you will have to fight for the change. It will not come easily and there is an uphill climb ahead of you. Many things will come to hinder you, you might fall back a little or for a short period of time, but fight for the change. Don't worry what people might think if you do slip back a little. Don't accept the fallback as defeat, get back on your proverbial horse and ride like you are armed for battle. Fight like your life depends on it, because it does.

By now, I am hoping you are getting a clearer perspective of how you got stuck. My hope is that you see that you don't have to stay stuck. The reality is you are where you are; but the truth is you can be in a different and better place. You can move on!

TWO
What is my Issue

Huh, an Issue? What do you mean?

We use the word a lot. We use it casually and seriously. We use it loosely and specifically. It seems to organically find its way into our daily conversations. Sometimes, we may even overuse it.

Let us consider a few ways we throw the word around.

What is the issue?

What is your issue?

Do you have an issue with me?

Wow, that person has got some serious issues.

You need to take the issue up with them, not me.

… Alright, I think you get the idea.

One time while I was waiting for a flight in the Dubai International Airport, I overheard a couple having a vigorous exchange of words. Ok, they were arguing! After a few moments of going back and forth in their native language to English, the lady blurted out in English, "You have got some serious issues!" She was so loud that several people turned and looked including me. What could she have been talking about I wondered?

It is safe to conclude that we all mean very different things when we use the term "Issue." Here are a few ways we use it.

If the issue is moral or spiritual, we are probably implying that the person is battling with a lack of character, values, decency, convictions or faith.

If the issue is financial, we are probably implying that the person is having challenges earning wages, maintaining their budget, saving, investing or maybe they are compulsive spenders with no clue how to steward their money.

If the issue is psychological, we are probably implying that the person is battling some type of disorder such as, Obsessive Compulsive Disorder, Post-Traumatic Stress Disorder, Compulsive Overeating or other disorders.

If the issue is relational, we are probably implying that there is relational tension, frequent disagreement and arguments, trust issues, or poor communication.

If the issue is professional, we are probably implying that there are serious concerns with landing a good job or career, avoiding unhealthy conflict with co-workers, or perhaps struggling to get your entrepreneurial ideas or business off the ground.

If the issue is medical, we are probably implying that the person has some sort of sickness, disease or permanent physical handicap.

We have all been in at least one of these categories a few times around in life. And while we usually ask the question referring to someone else, when was the last time you asked about your own issues? Have you ever asked yourself, "What is my issue?" Seems a bit odd doesn't it?

Perhaps it is not odd at all…

Let's face it, we know we have them. We would rather not talk about them. We sure aren't trying to put our private matters out on social media for everyone to know. So, we internalize a lot of personal issues until they eat away at the very core of our sanity. You know exactly what I'm talking about.

At the time of this writing, I am a new grandpa. I go by "Paw Paw." My goodness, I am loving every second with this precious little gift! I will try not to make this entire chapter about her — no promises — but, I will try hard not to!

My granddaughter's name is Majesty Nayeli and she has just turned ten months at the time of this writing. Majesty is a very active, jovial ten-month-old who is doing just about everything now. Her recent nine-month checkup revealed that she is testing far beyond her age.

When I learned this I wasn't surprised. I can barely recall a time that she has not been bouncing, jumping, laughing and loving her life! I was in the delivery room when she was born. She came out looking around. She was a caesarean birth. She was nosy — alright curious and inquisitive — looking all around as the nurses cleaned her up. One nurse said, "Her hearing was fine" as she was following the sound of voices so well — especially her mom's voice. As her mother called out to her from the other side of the room, she immediately looked in her direction. I kid you not!! It is awe-inspiring to watch Majesty in action now. She has continued her practice of being active from birth. She is a pure bona fide joy-maker!

My daughter still lives at home which means Majesty lives with us. So, I get lots and lots of quality time with her. I was warned by many veteran grandparents that I would be captured and enslaved by our grandchild. They were right! I am a prisoner to that little angel baby!

One of the wonderful joys I have had since Majesty has been with us is to take her to her doctor's check-ups. I have missed only one so far. I was traveling when she had to make an unplanned visit to the doctor. I try to make sure that her check-ups are scheduled when I am home because

I just have to be there. I never missed a single visit for our children, Walter III and Charity Ashely, and I am hoping to hold the record tightly for Majesty — at least through her first two years.

Ok, I am getting off subject now. I told you, I would try not to go on and on about her. And, I am trying… I am just not succeeding. Alright, you have to give me a small break! Anyway, your heart is probably melting as I talk about her. You've said "Awww" at least once, haven't you?

Back to the subject at hand.

Due to my daughter's work schedule, there have been a number of times I have taken Majesty to her doctor visits by myself. Oh, do I love it! A few of our visits were more than routine visits. Majesty has had a number of ear infections as a result of colds she caught from the rough 2019 winter we endured. She is also in the academy that her mom works at and it is likely that Majesty took a few bacterial hits from her sweet little playmates as well.

I recall one of her visits when we could not see her primary physician. She was booked to capacity the day we wanted to take Majesty in for a check-up. Due to her inability to see the baby, she recommended we should go to the Levine Children's Pediatric Clinic. This is a five-star day clinic for children which is also in the same medical network of Pediatric physicians.

I was so grateful that her doctor was able to find an opening there for Majesty as she had a relentlessly high fever, runny nose, flushed face, and a few other annoying symptoms. I had her checked in at the clinic and was told that a physician would see her shortly. In less than three minutes we were being called back to see the doctors.

After the typical exchange of pleasantries with the medical team, the doctor then asked, "Paw Paw, what seems to be the issue with our little angel baby today?" I gave him a brief account. I wanted to be quick but thorough as I was desperate to see her helped and pain-free. It was hurting me to watch her in pain. When our little ones hurt, we hurt too. If you are a parent or grandparent you can empathically relate to what I am saying here.

The doctor examined her. He listened to her heart, lungs, breathing, looked down her throat checked her ears and a few other routine things, then he looked up and said, "I know what the issue is. Your explanation of her symptoms and my examination reveals she has a double ear infection." Oh, can I tell you, my heart almost dropped to the floor! I was emotionally devastated because she had just gotten over an ear infection a month and a half prior to this visit, and now we were staring a double infection in the face. I had tears in the corners of my eyes but I held it together with strength from the Lord.

After talking over her medical issue, his diagnosis and how he was going to treat it, he stood and turned to me and said, "Thank you, Mr. Boston. It was such a pleasure working with you and meeting your granddaughter. You made this visit very easy and pleasant." I asked, "How so, doc?" He said, "Because you stated Majesty's medical issue so clearly, I was almost sure of her diagnosis before examining her. You made the process very easy."

I think you see where I am going with this. If you want to get unstuck from something and move on, you must state the symptoms causing the issues first.

What if I had rambled and not been clear about Majesty's symptoms. The doctor would have found out what was going on, but being clear about the issues aided him to diagnose and treat her properly.

When you are stuck state the specifics when asked, "What is your issue?"

Too often when people are asked how they are doing the reply is: "Oh, I'm ok, just got a few things going on." A few things… what are the few things? Being vague will not get you unstuck. Oh I know that sometimes we honestly may not know what is going on. At other times, we know, but we don't want anyone else to know.

When you are stuck, speak to the heart of the issue. It will be very helpful.

So let me ask you the question: What is your issue? What has you mired and glued in the sludge of life at present? The good thing is that you don't have to admit it to me face-to-face, but I would like for you to ask yourself and answer honestly if you can. If you don't know then do not fret as there is still help for you. If you really want to confront this matter head on, get in front of a mirror and ask the question out loud while looking directly at yourself, "What is your issue?" I know it's a little bold and possibly awkward, but hey, we are trying to get unstuck and an extra measure of effort may be perfectly in order. Don't mince words, don't try to sugar coat it and make it less ugly or less disappointing than it is, just be brutal and call it what it is. Remember your reflection has been sworn to silence! It will not hurt you!

Apart from circumstances in our lives beyond our control, I am going to spend the rest of this chapter addressing three specifics ways I have observed that many of us get stuck in life and cannot move forward. Not all of us, but most of us fall into one or more of these areas.

How do you and I end up with long-term moral, financial, psychological, relational, professional and medical issues?

Attractions

Most issues in our lives start with an attraction. What you focus on will inevitably manifest by experience. You gravitate towards what you focus on whether good or bad or somewhere in between. The first move we make is allowing it to be entertained in our thoughts. We are creatures of thought, hence always thinking. We think when we are awake. We think when we are asleep. Even when we turn our minds off, thoughts somehow creep in from somewhere. You probably have experienced this when you have ludicrous dreams that are comical and unsettling or both. We can't seem to turn them off! Experts estimate that we think approximately 60,000 to 80,000 thoughts per day. That breaks down to roughly 2,500 to 3,300 thought per hour! That is staggering just to know. It is like our minds rarely rest. It is important to point out that these estimations are for those who are not in overdrive in their thought life. If you are a person who lives their life in overdrive the numbers go way up.

Since you move towards what you are attracted to, this clarifies how you encounter most of your life situations. I know you have asked yourself a thousand times, "So when did we — my thought and the manifestation of that thought — meet?" In other words, where did this come from or when did it start. We generally chock life experiences up to happenstance or chance in our own minds, but there is such a depth to the attraction that we have towards certain things, and how the end results of that attraction manifest in real life. It all started way before it manifested, usually in the river of denial when you were thinking, and it was just a thought, nothing to lose sleep over, but nonetheless there in your gray matter. It had already began its combustion of becoming an attraction of the wrong kind, but of course the denial won't let any of us admit to it at this point. You have been titillated at this point, and it only grows from there.

I have already stated in chapter one that our thoughts lead to our behaviors.

One time I was checking out at a grocery store and decided to use a clerk instead of the self-check which is my normal routine as sliding bar-codes across those self-checkout machines is a lot of fun in my estimation. Besides, the grocery clerk was waiting for customers and looked bored out of his head! His body language was screaming at me to let him ring up my groceries the old fashioned way. So, my thought was to help this gentleman's day move along faster by going through the regular check-out.

We spoke to each other and got into a brief chat about the weather — you know the jargon — and before you knew it, he had swiped and bagged my few items. Then he asked me for my rewards number. While I was giving it to him, I pulled my card out to pay and remarked, "Wow we have so many PIN numbers to remember these days. Let me make sure I enter the correct PIN." I knew the PIN, but I was just holding a conversation with him because I could see it was as welcome as spring rain in a desert.

Would you know, within seconds, he looked up, smiled and said, "Sir, you entered the wrong PIN number."

If was funny. We both laughed! In my mind, I was thinking of a PIN number that I did not want to use and ended entering that very PIN. Although this was a very small error and easily correctable, it illustrates perfectly that what we focus on, we carry out effortlessly. I was sure I would be entering the right PIN, but my thought processes directed things otherwise as I was thinking of a PIN I DID NOT WANT TO USE.

Attractions are unavoidable, very natural and they vary in how they affect us. There are food attractions, people attractions, material attraction, popularity attraction and maybe one that is the biggest for most of us, sexual attraction. None of these attractions are bad in and of themselves, but they will quickly turn bad if we lean in excessively. One day, you look up and oh boy, you are stuck! You can't stop overeating, you are stalking someone in a bizarre and compulsive way, you can't stop swiping the credit card, you can't stay off of social media because you are posting for "likes" that are not the high numbers that you crave for, or you end up in some sexual relationship that isn't moral. Suddenly the tables are turned and now what you went after is coming after you. It has you stuck and you are struggling to move on.

One of my favorite scriptures, since my childhood has been, James 1:14 which says, *"We are tempted by our own desires that drag us off and trap us"*. As a teenager in Christ, I wrote this scripture in the front of my Bible and read it daily so that I could be reminded to avoid — as best as I could — my own *traps* or you could say attractions. There were successful days and not so successful days. I still work on not being dragged into traps that will hold me back or get me stuck. There is something persistent about our fallen humanity that is attracted to folly. It is in all of us — even the strongest among us. Once we are attracted, if we are not careful, it will leave us stuck, it can be the superglue of life!

Addictions

If you are not careful, before you know it, your attractions will turn into addictions. This happens when issues have gone way too far and you are no longer the one in control. Losing control is never planned but it happens.

Most of us believe that when we move towards something — whether good or bad — that we have it all under control. And this is true for the most part, at least at the beginning. When we first become involved in the dalliance, we work the situation like a pro. However, over time, the authority begins to change. You are no longer calling the shots and you can't seem to do anything about it. It is said, *"When you can stop, you don't want to. And when you want to stop, you can't. That's addiction."* This is a nightmare of a place to be stuck in. Furthermore, most of us can't fathom not being in control — right? We live to control, it is human nature and only true reliance on God can control this human need to control.

I will never forget a cold Monday in late 2014 as I was walking through Munich International airport in Germany. I was on my way to my terminal to catch my final flight home. I had served across four European nations over a period of thirteen days and had taught upwards of forty times or more. I was physically and mentally spent. I had an epiphany to turn my cell phone off while waiting in the terminal for my flight home as this would allow me an hour and half of extra quiet and reflective time to meditate on the goodness of the Lord in my life. I was going for the extra quiet time because I had already budgeted my ten hours on the plane to watch two comedy movies, write two articles and catch up on my sleep. Comedy movies are therapy for my soul and sleep keeps me looking good. I'm just kidding about the looking good remark! I really wanted time with the Lord to thank Him for the opportunities He gives me to represent Him. I love to hang out with Him in fellowship — just Him and me alone.

As I reached for my phone to put it in the "do not disturb" mode, a call appeared on the screen. When I looked, I was very shocked at who it was. At first glance, I didn't think I was seeing it correctly so I stopped walking and looked again. It was my first cousin Al, whom I had grown up with. I was shocked to get his call because we had not spoken frequently over the years since becoming adults. There was no stress or strain in our relationship, it was just that life had taken us in very different paths which caused infrequent conversations.

As a pre-teen, I came to faith in Christ and followed the path of discipleship with passion until this very day. My cousins Al and his now deceased brother Randychose a different path. They got caught up in the street life, theft, drugs and frequent visits to the county jail. It was really a hard thing to watch this happen. Both of the brothers were in jail early on in their lives. This cycle did not stop; it spiraled downhill landing both of them into the field of being career criminals with destructive addictions. Much of their time was spent incarcerated.

Al was calling me because he wanted to share something miraculous that was happening in his life. As a result of his past life, he had fallen prey to drug addiction which fatally ruined just about every other area of his life. He went on to share many of the details about his life that I didn't know. I knew the ugly results as they were public for all the family to see, but I didn't know the details that lead to the path of destruction he had been on. As he shared his testimony, tears poured from my eyes and would not stop.

First, I was so overjoyed to hear from him. Secondly, I was glad to hear what I was hearing from him. He was giving me the testimony of how his life was changing and that at the age of 49, he was finally breaking free from drug addiction, regaining a relationship with his adult son whose life he had not been a part of, meeting his grandson and getting a job as a chef at a restaurant. He was happy that he had just opened his first bank account in his life! The new job as a chef was his first public job since he was a teenager because his prior record made him unemployable. He had worked private jobs and side gigs in New York for a living.

As he continued to share, more tears poured profusely down my cheeks. I couldn't stop crying as I listened to him talk. I am sure the other passengers in the airport lounge were thinking to themselves that I must be getting some really bad news. The opposite was true — I was getting some really, really great news! It was mind blowing, heart-moving news!

And then suddenly, in a moment, the phone went silent and he said, "Junior — my family refers to me as Junior or Walter, Jr. — I want to tell you one last thing." I said, "Yes, I am listening." He said, "You know me, Randy and the boys (referring to our childhood friends) watched how you went hard after the Lord when you were a kid. You were always that little preacher boy for the whole neighborhood! We all had the same opportunity to stay in the church and follow the Lord because we were brought up like that. I remember like yesterday how we would get in the backyard and play church. You would be the preacher and we were the choir and the congregation. Boy, those were the good old days. You took that stuff for real, but me, Randy, and the others made some very wrong choices that messed us up for a long time!

I just wanted you to know that since I have been clean for almost one year, I decided that I needed to get my life back on track. So, the other day, I went to Pastor Donnie McClurkin's church because it is just down the block from where I live. When Donnie started singing and preaching it took me back to those days in Little Raleigh." This was the community where we were raised in Eastern North Carolina. He went on to say, "I decided during that service to give my life back to Christ. I ain't trying to play with the Lord, 'cause I know better. I just asked him to help me to stay straight and clean so I can be there for my son, my grandson, my new girlfriend and for myself. I didn't want to lose them anymore."

Well, it was then that I started sniffling out loud before I knew it. I was totally wrecked and beaten in that airport lounge and no one was hitting or hurting me. My cousin was sharing his story of deliverance and freedom from a life of addiction — thirty-four years of it — and I was trying not to make a swimming pool in that room and drown me and everyone else in my river of tears.

I remembered saying in a trembling voice to Al that day, "Man, today you are back in the driver's seat of your life. You ain't stuck no more and now you can move on from the past — hallelujah!"

He asked me if I was ok because he could hear the trembling in my voice as I spoke. I assured him I was fine and we affirmed our love for each other and agreed to keep in touch more often. We ended the call and that's when I put the phone in the do not disturb mode, left the lounge and went to the main hall of the terminal building that I was in and ran back and forth a few times giving thanks to the Lord. Now I did it in a way not to draw attention to myself. I was in an airport and I wasn't trying to get the attention of airport security. They are watchful and don't play around if they have so much as a question about a passenger's behavior. They will be on you faster than fast! In fact, most people who saw me trotting probably thought I was trotting to get to another terminal, but I was running and doing a happy dance in my head. All my fatigue left me that morning, I was instantly renewed and refreshed. It was as if I had not worked at all!

I do not know where you are in this season of your life or what you might be addicted to. But, I want to assure you of one thing, if your attraction has led to addiction — maybe even a long term addiction like Al experienced, you can get unstuck and move on just as he has done!

By the way, since that time, Al has moved from New York back to North Carolina. He has gotten a new lease on life. He is living drug-free, has a good relationship with his family and is enjoying his best days doing things he never thought he could do. I am so proud of him and grateful for his life!

Affection

This is the last area that I have noticed that often leaves us stuck, or in the words of the James the Apostle, "Trapped."

If we don't properly manage our attractions they will turn to addictions and if we are not careful, our addictions will turn to affections. You know this is happening or has happened when you fall in love with the very thing you have become stuck on and can't break free from although it has you in shackles.

It is hard to understand or explain why we have such a natural draw towards things that are not good for us. The crazy thing is that the things that are not good for us are all too often the apple of our eye in our own minds, but definitely not good for us whatsoever. Before you know it, we are loving something that is destructive to our lives. Man, this has happened to me so many times! The Apostle Paul had this challenge as well. He admits to it in Romans 7: 19-20 in the Bible. When we fall in love it is not easy to get over it even if it was very wrong from the start!

I have walked confidentially with thousands of people from all walks of life in private matters and have found that no one is immune from loving things we shouldn't love. No matter your status or class in life, we all have affections that are ready to attach themselves to something or someone. We are all given to our emotions. When our emotions escape from inside of us to interactions with people and things that is when we become bound to affections that drive us. We may drive them for a while, but left unchecked, they will take the driver's seat and drive us in ways so that we lose control.

Since affection can be given and received this makes it very possible to connect on an emotional level even if you don't consider yourself an emotional person. Have you ever said, "I am trying to move on but my feelings are shackling me to this situation or thing!" This is emotion sitting in the driver's seat.

As I write this I am thinking of several times in my life when I was trapped, stuck and couldn't move on because my emotions kept getting the best of me. I knew that I needed to get out of stuck mode, but when my feelings kicked in, I would go back to the very thing that was holding me hostage. When you and I get stuck emotionally — our affections get locked onto something like an impenetrable chamber or the vice grip of a crustacean which can hold on with a force that could cause major damage— and it becomes very difficult and challenging to depart or detach from their clutches or to move on.

Please understand that I am not saying that affections or emotions are bad — they are not. To be able to feel is a gift from the Lord. We are told to use them to build healthy relationships.

Helen Keller was an American author, political activist, and lecturer who left us with some wonderful written treasures. Both deaf and blind from birth, she accomplished much in spite of her handicap. She beautifully penned the following: *"The best and most beautiful things in the world cannot be seen or even touched. They must be felt with the heart"* Oh how I agree so much with this!

Remember, I started this book communicating to you that getting stuck starts directly with our thoughts. Several times, I will refer to this reality in the book. Please pardon my redundancy. I just don't want you to miss this vital truth. Nothing in the world is more powerful than our thoughts. Everything begins there! Even our affections are controlled by our thoughts. This means bad thoughts can produce bad affections, while good thoughts can produce good affections. We call this the law of attraction. Please don't confuse this with the New Age teaching of the laws of attraction to get wealth and power, I speak of a very different thing here. If we are not watchful, our affections will imprison us or free us. The choice we make determines the results or attractions we end up with. Bottom line, we don't want to remain stuck in something purely based on our emotions as emotions alone are not complete. Being led by emotion makes you a person without thought, logic or order. You chase the wind, doing whatever you feel, without thought of consequences or ripple effects it might cause. This way of living is not healthy by any certainty.

I have seen this play out tragically in personal and professional relationships. I have seen the downfall of good people. I have watched misplaced affections trap people in fatal relationships wherein they didn't just lose stuff, some lost their very lives. Suicide is at an all-time high in our society because people are struggling to gain control of their misplaced affections. If you are on social media or watch the news, you see this societal tragedy almost daily. It is causing a swift and sorrowful collapse in our society.

It is almost impossible to read this part of the chapter without deep thoughts and self-reflection. In fact, it is highly likely that even now you are having thoughts about how you are stuck in something and your affections towards it are winning over your sound reasoning about it. It is a tug of war that you can't seem to win. It is back and forth, back and back, and it is stressing you out. It is taking a toll on your life and eating away at your sanity. It may also be contributing to a family break-up, or a life of disorder and sorrow.

Listen, you can get control over this area and together we will!

In the coming chapter, I will address in detail how to gain the so-desired control. But for now, I want you to read this with an attitude of hope all the while admitting where you are and focusing on where you want to be.

May this very moment begin a new walk forward for you, one step at atime.

THREE
I am Stuck
Because of Hurt

Emotions show up in every facet of our lives. They don't wait for our invitation; they are intrinsically there. They are there for everything. You can see them, hear them and of course feel them. Sometimes, because they appear so suddenly and unannounced, we try to suppress or hide them. We are often shocked by their rudeness especially when it is a negative emotion.

How you feel is how you feel. Whether it is right or wrong, good or bad, your feelings are your feelings and while some will tell you to get over it, or that you are wrong to feel that way, your feelings encamp about you until such time they are ready to leave, usually after healing. Pastor and Author, Rick Warren says, *"Revealing your feelings is the beginning of healing!"* That's good truth there!

You are familiar with emotions such as happiness, sadness, anger, fear, worry, grief, regret, bitterness, loneliness, worthlessness, and helplessness to name a few. You have already met them on a personal basis. So I don't have to teach you that when emotions are felt, they are felt and sometimes felt overwhelmingly. Malcolm Gladwell, staff writer for the New Yorker, takes my thought a step further and says, "Emotion is contagious."

What?

I say we see them, hear them, know them and feel them and Malcolm says you can catch them too! No doubt you have experienced this with persons who share your space: if someone exhibits bad behavior or moods around you and others in your circle, generally everybody is affected by it, especially the ones who are close to each other. These emotions seem to be absorbed by osmosis, whether good or bad. Maybe you had not given this much thought before now but joy and sorrow, anger, frustration, etc. can be caught and multiplied to everyone that it swoops and circles around like a vulture on its prey.

By now you may be thinking, whoa, just reading this is disconcerting and will cause an emotional attack. That is not what I am trying to do to you. Stay with me because you have this book for help. I promise to help you not hurt you--although it may hurt to help you! This will be like when you visit the doctor's office and he pokes you in order to diagnose you. The poking is very uncomfortable and often painful but the end results are worth the poking.

So when you consider the brief list of emotions I have provided for you — and this is not all of the known emotions we experience — the negative ones outnumber the positive ones on the list I have provided. Not to worry there are plenty of positive ones I assure you.

I am not a clinical psychologist, I am a pastor and friend to leaders. I have nine years of collegiate disciplines in subjects such as theology, missiology, and trends of secular and sacred leadership and a few others. I also have a two-year certification in family counseling but I am not a licensed counselor.

However, I can honestly say that after forty-one full-time years of loving and leading people from all walks of life, I have a thing or two I can share with you about emotions. I have met all of them in my sessions. In fact, I have learned a lot more than I have been able to teach in forty-one years of being in the people business. The people business is all I have ever done. It is all that I know. And one thing I have learned and seen time and time again is that no one has ever shown up in a session without their emotions. They never check them by the door. Many have shown up motionless and stoic, but never without their emotions.

By the Lord's grace and help I have counseled with men and women of the highest offices in the world, folks from all professions and also the everyday people, and not a single one was ever present without their emotions. Plenty of folks have attempted to hide them, cover them and even deny their emotions. It never works as ultimately the emotions appear. They most certainly can be rude so let me share what I have consistently seen.

While I do very little counseling these days and more mentoring and fathering, what I have seen over four decades and still see now is that most people will come ready to unpack their issues. Remember, we taught in chapter two how issues can be wide-ranging. So just think of all of those and more! There is usually no shortage of hurts and issues. In fact, I think the list is ever growing, or least it seems that way.

My counseling sessions

My custom is to welcome the personto the session, briefly state my vow of confidentiality and then ask, "What is on your heart?" I spend forty-five to fifty minutes intently listening. I have tried over the years to listen with my ears and my heart. You will be amazed at what you will hear when you are present on both levels. I learned very early that the greatest need among people is to be listened too.

Once the person or persons are done sharing, I will ask, "So how do you feel about what you just shared?" The responses I have gotten through the years started to sound like the list of emotions I provided for you earlier in the chapter — mostly negative. I have heard it all from emotional and emotionless individuals.

The reality is that most folks are not just stuck on what happened or is happening to them. They struggle to get beyond how it is making them feel. This becomes a major issue as I will share in more detail in just a moment.

My notes over the years reflect that a very high percentage of the people who came in to talk needed to talk because they were stuck in hurt mode. A lesser percentage were stuck on the issue that caused the hurt. Most of us are hurt about something. I once talked to a young man who forgot the issue that led to his anger because he had obsessed about it all based on the amount of hurt it was causing for such a long time, that he forgot the root cause of it all. Anger had become his new normal and focus. When I asked "What are you angry about," he replied, "Just everything!" I asked, "What specifically started you down this path?" He said, "You know, I don't remember!" Do you have moments like that? You have been angry with a certain someone, and you have held the grudge so resolutely for years, but when you try to remember the cause of it all, that memory evades you.

So while I have listed a few emotions for you, all of which you have experienced in your life, I will focus on hurt in this lesson.

When you are hurt, disappointed and in disbelief because something has happened to you, or keeps happening to you — it hurts. You feel it. You don't ask to feel it, you wish you did not have to feel it, but you feel it. When we hurt in mind, soul, and heart, it is a different kind of pain. It is deep and often hard to explain. When the hurt lingers we waste away slowly in other areas including our physical and mental health. This is why we can't afford to leave hurt unaddressed.

Usually, I have only ten minutes to reply in a session. This is by design. There are times when I do not even use the ten minutes. Because when I ask, "How do you feel about what you just shared" they open up and the next ten minutes are used listening to how they feel. Most people will talk openly when they feel it is safe to do so.

I have ended many of my sessions by simply confirming what I heard, positively affirming them and praying for them. Then I will agree to meet again to listen and chat if they so desire.

Over the years it has been very moving to hear from individuals about their experience. It is common to receive an email, text, phone call, etc. stating how much the session helped. In the very early years when this happened, I would be awestruck at the comments and the positive outcomes.

In fact, I recall one time being so shocked by the message I had received from one person as to how I'd helped him and the surprise showed strongly in my facial expression. I was puzzled. My executive assistant asked me, "Pastor, are you ok; did I say something wrong?" I paused and looked with disbelief and asked her, "Are you sure this is what that person said?" She replied, "Yes! I wrote it down and I am reading it word for word exactly what he asked me to share with you."

The reason I was shocked was that I had listened to the gentleman for fifty minutes, affirmed him, prayed and ended the session. A short time later he called back and said, "It changed his life!" I was completely sold on my notion that the greatest need among people is to be listened to. I have taught my point exhaustively everywhere. It is always met with an immediate embrace by the majority in my audiences. The end of that story was that the person's private life, marriage, business, and walk with the Lord was all fully restored in a matter of months. He lived a very fulfilling and fruitful life until he passed from old age. He died a happy man. In fact, I remember at his funeral that he had a smile on his face. His wife told me that when he passed he was smiling. What a way to go out!

So let me ask you: Are you stuck on hurt?

Are negative emotions like sadness, worthlessness, helplessness, bitterness, etc. nagging and gnawing at you more than the issue that caused the hurt?

Do you feel low energy or no energy at all when the issue comes to mind?

Do you feel like you are trapped emotionally and can't find an escape?

Over the years in my follow-up sessions, I would discuss how we get stuck in hurt and how to get unstuck. I want to share some of this with you. Space will not allow me to share the full-length version, so an abbreviated version will have to do.

Please keep in mind I have no formal clinical training, so my observations are purely by reason of my pastoral and leadership experience. I share as a pastor and a friend. Some mental health clinicians may disagree with my approach and it's ok. I have had a high rate of success with this approach. Perhaps that will count for something.

I am addressing this matter of being "stuck on hurt mode" with emphasis because there is a prevailing cultural and popular belief that your feelings do not matter. How many times have we been told to get over our feelings? We hear stupid statements like, "You need to check your feelings at the door" or "Your feelings are going to get you into trouble so ditch them" and the list goes on.

I am not saying we should follow, be led or be controlled by our feelings or even trust them fully, but we have to acknowledge them and we have to listen to them.

How do we get stuck in hurt?

First, we get stuck in hurt when we push back our feelings. We push them away and say things like, "It is not important anyway. I will get over it." Remember what I have already taught you. We feel what we feel. Whether you know it or not feelings will not rest until they find a voice. Perhaps you had to push them back as a young child and have never learned to express them. That is why even when you are silent your feelings are still speaking to you in your head. If you don't give all of the churnings a positive voice, eventually it will assume its own voice and this is when things usually go towards the dark side. This is when anger, bitterness, and other emotions find a rather permanent lodging place. This is not healthy by any measure. If you speak to them by expressing them, they will find a positive outlet. This is where we fail in the process and issues are suppressed and they poison us.

Christian clinical psychologist, Henry Cloud says, *"Emotions, or feelings, have a function. They tell us something. They are a signal. Anger tells us that our boundaries have been violated. Much like a nation's radar defense system, angry feelings serve as an "early warning system" telling us we're in danger of being injured or controlled."*

Again, your feelings — no matter how much you try and avoid them — will not disappear until you speak up about them. I encourage you to speak truth to them. We will see the importance of speaking truth to them shortly. If they are talking to you, you will at some point have to talk back to them. Put it off now, but it will come up again later. Until you are willing to give voice to the hurt you feel it will not leave. It may go into silence, but the hurt will speak up again eventually.

Second, we get stuck in our hurt when we go into hiding. We will go along just to get along in public, but in private we hide and hurt. The wrong thing to do when you are stuck in hurt is to keep to yourself. Whoever suggested that you are all you need is sadly wrong. You will drown in self-misery if you go into long-term isolation when hurting. Being alone to think, process and clear your thoughts is good. It is also good when you want to rest. It is especially acceptable when you want to pray or meditate. On the other hand, hiding to avoid hurt is not good. Adam and Eve tried hiding in the beginning and it certainly wasn't successful. I have tried it and it wasn't successful for me. You have tried it — and let me guess — it has not been successful for you either huh? It does not work! The pain and even guilt will speak up so loudly that you will be grasping for sanity. If you retreat alone and hide, who will help rescue you? In chapter four, I will talk openly about the types of person you should talk to when you are hurting.

Third, we get stuck when we are at a loss for what to do or how to move on. Does this sound familiar? As if getting hurt wasn't devastating enough, we surely don't know what to do or where to go with hurt. It is very easy to feel paralyzed and confused emotionally in the heat of the hurting moment. It doesn't mean there is something wrong with you, but it is a tell-tale sign that something is seriously wrong somewhere. I experienced this painful feeling of hurt and gut-wrenching loss when my mother died. I had a series of moments were I was at a complete loss emotionally and mentally. I was stuck for a period of time. If you have ever lost a loved one, you understand this one with great empathy.

At this point in the river of pain, some might seek to medicate their feelings with excessive behaviors such as drinking and drugging in order to seek relief from the pain that has come knocking at the door. It is an incendiary stage which needs dealing with, not "forget your troubles, get happy" type of medication.

Fourth, we get stuck when we lie about how we feel. A definite way to stay in the trap is to be dishonest. Lying closes the door to receiving the help you need. It also locks you into an unreal and false world of beliefs and assumptions. What I have observed over the years is that if you lie long enough about something, you will eventually accept the lie as truth. I see this frequently in my sessions. Lying will trap you in your hurt. It will negatively compound the issue that you are dealing with. It is entangling enough to be fighting through vague and uncertain emotions. You would not want to add to that self-deception.

Jesus said, *"It is the truth that will set you free."* There have been many studies that show that lying repeatedly over time will dull your emotions and make you a slave to falsehoods. What this means is that over time you will adapt to the lie as though it is the truth. This is a trap. Many of us have been told things about ourselves from a very young age, things that destroyed us at the core of being, but because the person saying those things to us had a greater sense of authority, we accepted it as truth. This is how believing the falsehoods begins. It goes on long enough, and you hear it repeatedly enough that your own thoughts are lost in the mire of that falsehood. It is a difficult trap to escape from but it is possible.

Before I address how to get unstuck from hurt, take a moment and reflect on what you just read. If you are stuck in any of the four areas write down as much detail as you can about it. This is a good starting place in identifying what is really going on.

For the record, I have been trapped in all four areas at different seasons in my life. I can tell you they are cover-ups to get us to avoid the real issue. When we cover up we slow down our recovery. Tragically, we even prevent recovery when we fail to resolve the lies. Some people die and never address the hurt in their lives. This will not be you!

So let's look at the process I have developed for people to get unstuck from hurt. This is a very fundamental approach.

How to get "un-stuck" and free from hurt.

You *confess*. This is the first important step toward getting free. To admit that you are hurting and to agree that the pain is real will bring freedom and healing to your soul. When I speak of the soul, I am speaking of your mind and emotions. We had a saying in our church years ago that simply said, "Admit it so you can quit it!" The moment you agree to what is happening emotionally, you gain instant permission and power to do something about it.

The best way I can communicate this to you is to ask you to think back on when you were a child. You probably have plenty of memories of when your parents would ask, "Did you do it?" You, like most kids probably lied and said no. Then your parents would say something like, "If you tell the truth it will help you." You — scared out of your wits — came around and admitted it was you that had done the deed in question. And from there, mercy and grace were granted. Your behind and your pride might have been hurting for a bit but nonetheless you were corrected and freed to move on. This holds true in the matter of confessing hurt. Once you confess it and admit it, it positions you to move forward, to move on.

You *confront*. This is different in that you don't just admit the hurt, you address the hurt. You do something about it. You become the master of it rather than its slave. If we confess and don't do anything else, we are just talking. While talking is good as we have already taught, it is just opening the door. Confronting the hurt is moving into the inside of the room and dealing with the hurt. This requires courage.

Two years into my first pastorate in the early '80s, I found myself in a situation of deep hurt and betrayal. A pastor whom I trusted and respected greatly was blackballing me to others behind my back. This trusted friend and colleague had been responsible for helping me attain the position of senior pastor at the church I was serving in. He was on the board that recommended and approved my first senior pastorate. He was most gracious to provide a character letter for me and even to recommend some of my written work in basic Bible doctrine. This made me highly favorable with the church leadership in their decision to make me their senior pastor.

After a year of tremendous success at that church, he became jealous of me and began to speak lies about me to my board and ministry colleagues. The same board he spoke highly to about me, he was now sabotaging my name and leadership unjustly to them. After a short season of this nonsense, I called him and asked to meet with him. In our conversation, I bought the accusations and names of the persons he had been speaking to about my character to his attention and asked him if he had said those things. When confronted, basically he denied everything. When I offered to contact said persons on the telephone that he had disparaged me to, he then changed his tune and admitted to what he had done. We talked about it all, he asked for my forgiveness and I forgave him. As time passed, we did not have any dealings with each other. I had developed trust issues with him and his character had been tarnished in my eyes. I concluded that keeping a distance from the guy I'd forgiven was a wise thing to do. I forgave him, but I liked the idea of the brother staying away from me! In fact, I thought it was a God idea. You know what I'm talking about don't you?

A year later, I was having a large pastors and leaders conference. Everyone was excited because we were going to have delegates from many places across the United States and a few pastors were coming from international destinations as well. Things were coming together wonderfully and it was an exciting time of growth and leadership for the ministries I was allowed to steward. I had a vacant spot for one speaker that was not yet filled. I had prayed about who I could get to teach that seminar. I could not settle on anyone in my own right.

I decided to call another senior mentor to see if he was available to teach this session. I knew he was a busy itinerant speaker, but it was worth a try to ask. He was booked elsewhere but he had a recommendation for a speaker and was so ready to put that person's name forth. He said, "Have you considered asking… _______________." I think you see where this is going… the proposed speaker for this empty slot at the conference was none other than the name of the pastor who had blackballed me. He said, "He would be the perfect one to teach this course." I replied, "I'd rather not have him come teach at this time." He asked, "Why not?" I briefly explained to him what had happened a year before and stated that I thought it best that he not be invited.

I could hear a mild giggle on the phone and then silence for a few seconds. My senior mentor, with his baritone voice, gently said, "Walter, I did not know this and now that I do, I understand how you feel. However, if you really want to confront this matter and show that true forgiveness has taken place — invite him to teach. This will put to rest the hurt feelings of the past and bring sincere reconciliation." I asked my mentor, "Did you hear anything I just told you?He hurt me and lied about it. He almost cost me the church and more importantly, he tried to railroad my character." "Yes, I heard what you said, and it is good that you got him to confess it and you agreed to forgive him. But Walter, you haven't confronted your feelings on this matter. You confronted him, but you still live with raw and unaddressed feelings about it a year later. Put it to rest son. Invite him to teach. Have lunch with him before he teaches and confront your feelings of hurt and betrayal. Once you do this you will know that you are walking in Christ-like forgiveness, not your brand of forgiveness."

Whoa, that conversation that day really hit me smack in the face — right between my eyeballs! To be honest, I was now starting to feel a certain way about my mentor who was only trying to get me unstuck. It felt like he fell off his pedestal of being my mentor for a brief second. I initially thought he was being insensitive and dismissive. Was he trying to sabotage me too? But, after a moment of deep thought, I came to my senses and acknowledged that my mentor was right on this.

I had confronted how the brother had lied on me, but I had not confronted my feelings about it. An entire year had passed and I was still being very childish about the hurt I was feeling. I say this to teach you that when you do not confront your hurt feelings it will make you act childish and make you cynical. I think I just poked you. Stay with me, I am not trying to hurt you… I am trying to help you.

You can easily guess what happened next.

I ended my call with my mentor and called the pastor whom I had not released emotionally. We arranged to do lunch. During that luncheon, I confessed and confronted my emotional hurt. The moment I did, I felt a sense of instant freedom and reconciliation that I did not feel the first time we met. It wasn't him in bondage, it was me and I was so grateful to get it right and get free!

He accepted my invitation to teach at the conference. His session turned out to be one of the highest attended among our delegates. The leaders raved for months on about how they were helped and blessed by this guy. I almost prevented others from getting help because of my hurt. My right to hold on to the hurt could have been responsible for great loss and fall out in that it would have prevented a major blessing for the attendees at the conference. True forgiveness set me free!

This could not have happened if I had stopped at confession and not confronted my hurt feelings. I have implied this earlier, but I must repeat it again. If we are not careful we will allow our hurt feelings to become the main thing and overshadow the issue at hand. Today this brother and I are still good friends. We have ministered for each other on occasion. We actually like each other. No "Christian go-along to get along stuff" between us, just pure unity and acceptance.

You *cry*. You may be thinking... alright you were making perfect sense until this point.

CRY?!?!!

How does that help to get me unstuck?

Well, as weird as it may sound crying is a healthy and natural response to feelings of hurt and anger. Research has proven that when we cry we feel less sad. You may find it hard to believe, but it seems that the percentage is high in both males and females. In fact, studies have suggested and upwards of 87 percent of women and 75 percent of men felt less sad after a good cry. In addition, we know that crying releases stress, lowers blood pressure, detoxifies the body and the one that may not surprise you is that it helps us to embrace our feelings and emotions.

Crying is not a sign of weakness but rather, it is a sign of strength. It also tends to create a bond between the offender and the offended. This is really important.

In the Bible we see famous leaders and even kings crying. Esau, Joseph, Joseph's brothers, Samuel, and King David to name a few. We know that King David not only cried, but cried often because he was trying to address feelings of hurt that he had towards those who wanted him dead and even towards the Lord, whom he accused of not moving fast enough to defend him. David at times was an emotional wreck and he did not hold back the tears. Just read his journal of Psalms.

Jesus cried with great agony as well. He cried so hard for the agony he was undergoing, knowing full well that his destiny was the cross and crucifixion. So, there you have it, crying is ok! If you don't ever cry something is chronically wrong with you. You are internalizing your hurt and it is hurting you.

I cry! I cry alone. I cry around family. I cry around trusted friends. I cry in the presence of the Lord. I cry even if I don't want to at times. Oh, the refreshing I feel often when I am done crying is inexplicable in terms of relief. It is as if someone has lifted a trillion tons off my back. I go from feeling heavy to feeling light; from feeling weak to feeling strong; from feeling sad to feeling happy!

CRY! It is free. Try it soon. You can even do it now if you want too. It will be our secret. You can write me with a testimony about crying and how it helped you. And then, I'll start crying. See, it works!

You *commit*. As I have walked with thousands through their hurt; I have been very honest to share that in most cases moving on will be a journey. Therefore, I always ask if they are committed to the long haul of healing. This is important because you don't want to get up the road years later only to find out that you did not adequately address the process of time it takes to heal. Too many of us stand on our soapboxes and advise others to forget the hurt and move on, but do not let these types condemn you in the process of your healing. For years, you have let the hurts fester in your subconscious. Please understand this will not be an instant fix.

Healing from hurt is a journey of recovery. Rarely is it a one day trip. It is rarely a single act of recovery. There are those special times when the Lord does the miraculous and erases everything in one swipe. But in most cases, it's the Lord and others working for your recovery over time.

If this process is going to work for you, I am asking you to be committed to a number of things:

To the process of healing from the hurt

To the pain that the process may bring

To the price of brokenness that you will feel

To honest and full disclosure of issues

To the people who may be the culprits of the hurt

To the loved ones and professionals who are walking you through the hurt

To getting healed from the hurt no matter the length of time it may take

I have so much more I would like to write about on this subject. Perhaps someday, I will write on addressing hurts at full length.

For now, I close the chapter by adding one other thing that I know will be essential to getting unstuck. As a person of faith this is first in priority for me.

Prayer!

Listen!!! Please hear me out on this one. Prayer is really important and highly effective. If you are willing to share your honest feeling with the Lord, he will be there for you to help you process what to do. Remember, I stated earlier that many times we don't know what to do when we are hurting. The Lord knows what we need to do and will guide us through the process. I advise that you have many conversations with Him. Talk to him like you would any trusted friend. He is the best listener and a friend like no other. He emphatically understands, feels and knows exactly how hurt and betrayal work.

There is an abundance of scientific research which positively concludes that prayer (even as an experiment) helps people heal faster physically, emotionally and mentally. It was published in the Reader's Digest! Science is catching up to what the Bible has always taught us on this subject.

One of my favorite Bible verses is Jeremiah 30:17 which reads, *"I will restore you to health And I will heal you of your wounds, says the Lord!"*

I really wish I could unpack this verse for you. There is a ton of 'godly psychology' in this one — if there is such a thing! But, I must move on.

If you are reading this and you don't practice Christianity, I would still encourage you to talk to the Lord! Just try it on the basis of scientific research. If you struggle with faith or you are a practicing atheist then do it on the premise of being exploratory and experimental. It will not hurt or harm you. You may be wonderfully surprised how it will help.

I am believing with my heart that you are finding a place of hope and getting unstuck.

Yes, you!

You are on a genuine and doable journey of healing from emotional hurt.

And it is because you refuse to be stuck!

FOUR
I Need to Talk
to Someone

Only a fool speaks all his mind and while you may consider yourself an open book, your pages need not be read by everyone you meet. You cannot talk to everybody about your personal issues! This statement comes as no surprise to you. In fact, I'm willing to bet you an apple — my favorite morning fruit — that you have tried talking to a few people and it turned out to be the worst mistake ever! Alright, if not the worst, very close it!

There is a reason why we hide and retreat within ourselves when we are hurting. We don't trust ourselves in those vulnerable times; and we don't trust other people to understand or handle what we are dealing with. Therefore, we do what comes natural —- we withdraw.

Yet, it is clear that everybody needs somebody to confide in or to have as a sounding board. This is one of the basic needs of life. It is essential like the need for water, air, food, love, hope — you get the point. No one is excluded.

Author and professor, Gretchen Rubin says, *"We need to have intimate, enduring bonds; we need to feel that we belong, we need to be able to get support, and just as important for happiness, to give support. We need many kinds of relationships, for one thing we need friends"*

When I first read Gretchen's statement it prompted a number of immediate questions in my mind. I want to ask you my questions before we move further.

Do you recognize a need for others?

Do you bond in friendships or bow out?

Do you have a sense of belonging or alienation?

Do you feel supported?

Do you believe in the necessity of relationships?

Do you have a trusted friend?

Are you a trusted friend to someone else?

If your answers to more than the majority of these questions is "Yes" then I know you have a safe place to confide the deepest secrets or experiences in your life.

If your answers to more than the majority of these questions are "No," then I know you are in great need.

There may not be a person you feel safe talking with and confiding in.

If you have ever told someone a secret and they told someone else, you still remember the betrayal to this day. You don't want to hear from that person again, and if a thought of them ever floats into your mind, you rehearse the betrayal they are guilty of. You may have shared a thousand wonderful memories of doing life together, but depending upon what confidence was shared out of turn, it may have left you with feelings of deep regret and extreme embarrassment. Not everyone is built to keep a confidence. It is crucial to understand the role that each person will play in your life. If you miss this point you can very well end up in an overwhelmingly big mess. Please listen when I tell you that people messes are very complicated to clean up. They require a godly HAZMAT — hazardous materials — type of cleanup of things that have posed a risk to health or property or character or to the moral fiber of our being. HAZMAT teams work quickly to minimize the effect of the incident. Their techniques include containment of the crime scene, and securing all of the areas to keep destruction at bay.

I say that there are three kinds of people in your life.

Leakers. These people drip-drip-drip like a faucet that needs a new seal. Not long after you confide in them, they go merrily on their way to tell someone else and usually they do so at lightning speed. In the church community they preface their "juicy tidbit" of news with "don't tell anyone, but I am sharing this with you so that you can pray about it." Their sole intent is to pass the gossip along and enjoy the rush of sharing a juicy tale of gossip as well as doing their Christian duty of bringing everything to the Lord in prayer, albeit with a very insincere heart. Added to this breach of trust, they rarely confide the information correctly making matters worse. Do you remember playing the game of telephone in elementary school where the news was passed along quietly from the first person in the class and that person would whisper it to the next person and when it got to the tail end of the class, it did not even resemble the original piece of information. That is how the leaker types operate and they are labelled by me as trust-breakers.

Storers. These are people who will listen intently while you pour out your heart and soul. They will appear to be very safe, interested and compassionate. They download and store every word in their memory bank. At some future time when you would least expect it, like an opportunist they will bring up what you have shared and share it inappropriately with others and may again use the "would you pray about this" as a preface to this insidious gossip. They appear to be caring and spiritual and but are providing a grandstanding entrance for a topic that should not be shared. Some do it for vengeful reasons, others because they like to instigate. Their eyes dance with glee when they are sharing this privileged information. They get such a rush from this inappropriate behavior. These persons are labelled quite appropriately as trust-destroyers.

Holders. These are the people who gladly have you confide in them and they hold it. They don't tell anyone for any reason. They know the meaning of confidentially and they honor it. They will defend you privately and publicly. They are the trustworthy.

So please allow me to repeat my opening line to this chapter and I desire to expand on it by adding another line. I opened the chapter by saying, "You cannot talk to everybody about your personal issues." I want to add to this, "You should not talk to everybody about your personal issues."

In a world of increased social media this has become a very destructive habit for far too many. Too many people use this platform to vent their private issues. When the comments and replies begin to roll in, their emotions begin to flair in anger or desperation and the fight is on. Some have even taken their lives due to bullying on social media. YOU SHOULD NOT TALK TO EVERYBODY ABOUT YOUR PERSONAL ISSUES!

Transparency, honesty, and being real are all important, but in the right place with the right people and the right boundaries.

Alright, we'll move on from this point. I think you hear me.

Just who should you bare your heart to?

In the earlier years when I lead my church staff, we held regular meetings which we called "Pastor's Review." Those scheduled meetings were much anticipated times by the staff and me. Every Tuesday and Friday morning we would spend the first hour of our work day reviewing a Bible lesson, our weekly staff agendas for each department, and I would always present a seven minute leadership chat. Leadership has always been big on my priority list since that is my forte. I guided my church staff, and focused on broadening the leadership aspect for each of us in the team, as we are all called to be leaders in our own right.

One morning, I had to do a little pastoring with my staff, if you know what I mean. There were a few matters that had been grossly mishandled and I needed to give voice and correction to it.

On this day, I asked the team to come to the conference table with a blank sheet of paper and a red pen. When we gathered, we continued in our established custom: we prayed, read scripture, had everyone share a little on how they and their families were doing, reviewed our department agendas, and then I took to the floor to do my seven minute leadership chat.

I asked everyone around the table to print in upper case letters four words with their red pen: CHARACTER, CAPACITY, COMPETENCY AND COMMITMENT. Once they all were done writing and the red ink popped on their pages, I then opened my teaching with this line, "When you come to this table always come with these four things. Never come without them. If you neglect to bring these four items with you and within yourself, we will not be able to talk."

Everyone looked at each other and then back at me with a look of astonishment. They indeed were stunned. They knew that the teaching that day was not just a leadership chat, but a rebuke. You see, it came to my attention that a few of the team members had talked outside of our staff meeting about some highly confidential information that should not have been mentioned outside of our group. In fact, we were working on a few great and wonderful new opportunities for the church, but they were all in exploratory mode. Only the Elders and Executive Board members knew of this and we unanimously agreed to share it with the staff as they too would be seeing the communication coming into our office via emails, phone calls, letters, fax transmissions etc. and it would not be fair to them to be kept in the dark about it all. This mention of fax machines may bring a smile to your face as they are so outdated. And yes, although very outdated in 2019 in terms of technology, fax machines were at the forefront of technology in the 90s.

That day the team learned a valuable lesson. They were hit head on with the reality that although I was willing to talk and share, the scope of my sharing was only to a very particular type of person. Character, capacity, competency and commitment were paramount qualities and values in my trusted person type. For the next four meetings, each and every team member had to give their understanding of each of these words and why it was important to possess these attributes as a staff member. It was heartmoving to see the way they replied and instant apologies resounded around the table that day. I remember this like it was yesterday. We never ever had that issue again within the team. And whenever new staff members were added to the team, one of the core requirements of utmost confidentiality was drilled into the prospective staff member at their interview as a result of this meeting. Do you see where I am going with this?

I have also encouraged this method in personal relationships as well. If a person does not have character, capacity, competence and commitment, then you should not be so quick to talk personal or confidential things with them. Time and time again, I have seen people talk to the wrong people only to be disappointed that they were confiding in a "leaker" or a "storer."

Before we move on this is a good place for you to give thought to the people that you confide in. Do they possess these attributes? If not, I would advise and caution you to bump down your personal, private chats with them. Chances are if you have been speaking with them for a time now they have already leaked your confidence to someone who should not have those details on you. Everyone has a best friend who has a best friend. "Leaker and storer" types of people will spill it to their friends and anyone else who will listen!

I am not suggesting that you cut the person or persons off. I am simply advising you to be wise in what you share with them. Keep the conversation general and pleasant. Don't privy them to an insider track of the personal and private details of your life.

If you already have people who possess these four attributes in your inner circle, you are in good shape and you run much less of a chance of being hurt.

Now that we understand the attributes of the people you want to share deep things with, let's have a look into who they should be.

I have categorized people into six functional areas in my life: Models, Mentors, Counselors, Spiritual Fathers/ Mothers, Associates and Friends. This has allowed me to understand with a sense of clarity and ease who will be placed in different compartments of my life and how to align my relationships with them. Relationships that are not properly aligned will run like a car that needs a wheel alignment. It will tremble, roll roughly and steer in the wrong direction sometimes causing casualties in its path.

As I have matured over the years this list has certainly become very defined and refined for me. This book does not allow me to teach exhaustively about the layers of relationship beyond these six. But I know these will be more than adequate to point you in a healthy and happy direction. I know this by reason of time and experience.

Let me briefly share with you how I have viewed and related to these people. After that, discussion in detail will follow to show how this can work when you need someone when in crisis or let's just say, "stuck" and can't move on.

Relationships.

My Models. These are people I may or may not know personally. Most of them influence me from a distance. I see good traits in their lives that I am attracted to and I will incorporate them into my life without losing my individuality. A wonderful spiritual father and author, Jack R. Taylor often says, "Be you because it is the only person that is not taken." Don't you just like that? It is a great nugget of truth! So, I never change my personhood to be like someone else, but I will make the qualities they possess mine and model them through my unique personality. These are not people I share personal deep things with. I just admire something about them that can work for me.

My Mentors. These are people I am familiar with. We most likely know each other on a first name basis. Our relationship is usually cordial and casual. I learn certain skills, practices, and proficiencies that they have perfected — areas that they may be experts in. I am mentored by them through their books and media resources. I may even be fortunate to meet up with them in person on occasion. I ask lots of questions as you have seen by the first few chapters of this book. I will ask questions for the purpose of personal growth and development. It is one of the most effective ways to learn. I rarely share deep personal details with this group.

My Counselors. This is the person whom I will turn to for my emotional and mental health. The relationship is usually professional. They generally are clinically certified counselors who can bring a deeper understanding of the emotional and mental issues I may be battling with. Often, I have used counselors who value Scripture so that their perspective is tied into biblical truth also. I have used non-Christian counselors and do not oppose using them. We can learn and be helped from anyone. I encourage a broad range of professionals in your life. Because clinicians are sworn to privacy oaths, I will share deep issues empowering them to provide adequate emotional care. This sort of intervention has saved me from crashing many times over.

If you are a person of faith reading this with strong personal convictions about receiving counsel only from the Bible, church leaders or others in your faith community please let me emphasize once more that seeking counsel from multiple sources is advantageous.

I sincerely applaud the counsel you will seek out from your circle of faith — don't stop doing that. However, if your situation is clinical in nature, such as depression or you are experiencing other pathological issues, you should seek the help of certified professionals who can adequately treat those identified issues also. There is no point in playing one professional against another. Let each professional — spiritual and secular — play their respective role in helping you. This will be a replete win-win for you!

My Spiritual Fathers & Mothers. These people relate on an intimate level with me. I know them personally, they know me personally. They care for my spirit and soul. They make sure that my spiritual, personal, and family life is functioning properly. I will speak with them frequently to provide them with a status report of how things are in my life. They hear the deep, private, ugly and embarrassing stuff and help me process and live through those seasons. They are parents in every sense of the term. They love, correct, chastise, celebrate, champion and carry me. They also help me bridge the gap between the mental and emotional care and the soul and spiritual care of both myself and those entrusted to me.

My Associates. These people are the everyday common folk whom I may know and chat with about things like the weather, current events, technology, etc. They are colleagues and peers and they are not ranked any higher than that in my trusted friend portfolio. We associate by reason of a common profession and participation. I may know them from the gym, library, church, community, the local store, etc. I have several good neighbors who fall in this category as well. My community is a good ethnic mix and it is enriching and fun to associate with people from all backgrounds. We may know general details about each other, but this is not the group that I would share deep, personal private things with. We just associate around the niceties of life.

My Friends. These are people who have made it to the inner circle of my life. However, not all of them rank the same. This is important to note. Hear me when I tell you: not all your friends are ranked at the same level or position in your life. If you don't know this, you can end up confiding in a friend who is a leaker or a friend who is a storer. Be wise! Just because they are considered a friend doesn't mean they possess our four "Cs". …You know the ones that say, if you have these we can talk!

For example: your spouse or significant other would rank on the intimate level of friendship or at least they should. If they don't… well, that's another book. Your best friend would rank on the intimate platonic level of friendship. You may share some of the same deep, personal, private matters with them, but you will not cross moral lines with them. This is imperative to point out because often where there is intimate chatting about life, intimate feelings can find their way into the mix. Your casual friends will share some closeness and endearment with you, but this is where there would be selective sharing. Not all of your casual friends will be holders. If they are not, just be casual and loving.

Now you have insight of how people are ranked in my life. I trust this is helpful to the question of "With whom do I share my innermost thoughts and concerns with?" Now permit me to share with you the group from this list that I confide my deepest, private and personal wins, losses, successes, defeats and other information not found in this list.

I will have my deepest conversations with my friends of the most intimate level and a different depth of intimacy is held with my intimate platonic friends. It is with this group of the most intimate level that I feel more than friendship, I feel covenant friendship. When I am in need, or if they are in need, we can come to one another's rescue at the drop of a coin. We ask questions later but we rescue first. Please note that having such friends need to be a two way highway, not a one way thoroughfare. By this I mean if you are doing all the giving and never receiving, there is cause for concern or vice versa. Many a manipulative, narcissistic, self-serving person has impersonated an altruistic true-blue friend and taken the unwittingly trusting soul to the proverbial cleaners, so let me implicitly state that your discernment and intuition need to be turned on full-force as even the most discerning person can get sucked in by the wolf in the altruistic friendship sheep's clothing. Be wise, have your feelers cocked and your gut feeling honed to the nth degree in these situations.

Many times this small group of people have talked me off the cliffs of life. They have helped me not to commit ministry or leadership suicide. They have kept me from my own folly. They have loved me in my weakest moments of failure and disappointment. They have been there and are still there unconditionally. Their love, integrity, selflessness, truth, compassion, heart, and more is a life source to my hurts. The Lord uses these men and women powerfully in my life. I can only hope that I am this to someone also. One last truth, these relationships are often lifetime relationships. Whether you meet them early in life or late in life they stay with you 'til the very end.

There are people whom I walk with like this and their personal and private hurts and/or failures will go with me to the grave. I will never, ever utter their confidences to anyone but the Lord. You will not see their personal details on display in one of my books or sermons, in a public prayer request or a testimony. I will keep their confidence to the grave.

Sometimes when hurts have lingered, such as when my mother died, it was just a few choice people that helped me live through the trauma of that season. Even now that Mom has been gone for a decade, I still hear from two of my friends every year on her "life-a-versary"— the anniversary of her passing into eternal life. They will say, "I know what day today is Walter, how are you doing?" They won't let me internalize or get stuck in the hurt that comes when we lose a loved one.

I want to talk about you now. You didn't think I'd let you slide did you? I want to talk to you. We have already agreed that in some way we are all stuck in life. You may be working through mild or major hurts at the reading of this book. You may have come of out a situation and you are trying to clean and tidy up the fall-out of the repercussions surrounding it. Whatever the case… I want to talk to you!

Who are you talking or bearing your soul to?

If your answer is, "I keep it all to myself where it is safe." I have to be honest and say to you, you are killing yourself and there is nothing safe about internalizing hurt and pain. It is sorrow, and sorrow is not safe; it burrows and digs at your inner core and makes a shell of you and all you are supposed to be. At some point, you will become so hollow you will snap like a twig under the tiniest gust of oppressive wind. You need to get trusted people into the inner circle so you can receive the care you need for your emotions, mind and soul.

Chances are there are people who already qualify for this role in your life. At the time of this writing there are approximately 7.53 billion people in the world. There has to be at least one out of this number who understands your hurt; who will gladly help bear your pain. You have to look for them. And they are probably looking for you. And once again, it is kindof hard to be found if you are hiding.

How to make good friends.

Friends will usually show up in one of the following ways:

Casual meet and greet events. There are those rare times you speak to someone and instantly you get a good vibe about the person. You are not sure what it is but you feel a sense of familiarity, a desire to get to know them a little better, maybe even build a possible friendship. Ask them to go for coffee or lunch to get acquainted. If they live in a different place, ask to speak with them on one of the popular chat apps. I have become a model and mentor to people all over the world this way.

Spiritual, social and sporting events. So many good friendships form around church, small study groups, golf, football, tennis, running, hunting, fishing, and other social events. When you share the same hobbies and passions, they tend to connect you at deeper levels. One of the spiritual sons that I care for now, I met at a gaming center called The Sports Connection. It is a place that has all kinds of games, and fun things to do. It's really great for family outings too. The one that I go to has a bowling lane and laser tag. I like bowling and laser tag a lot! I'm not that good at either, but it is good therapy for me. Hitting those pins, and shooting my targets with laser lights often relieves stress.

One day I got so many strikes while bowling that a young fella playing beside me asked, "How did you get so good at bowling?" I smiled and said, "I am not good at it, I am just having a good day!" We started a conversation from there. The next week he found me online and sent me a message. He said he needed a spiritual father and he knew I was the man. Here it is, a great relationship born from the great sport of bowling, and I can't even bowl that well. Not a bad deal at all!

I know many people who have formed bonds of friendship because they went through similar life changing events or life situations. These relationships are often born at the doctor's office, hospitals, cancer treatment center, or while enrolled in substance abuse care programs, and sometimes even through the loss of a loved one. You can forge a bond with a friend for life when you both have experienced agonizing loss and grief. You go on to cope and conquer grief through the bond of friendship that is born out of tragedy as nobody knows the depth of your pain as the ones who have lived through it in a similar vein.

At work. Sometimes a co-worker may change their status in your life from associate to friend. Usually this bond of friendship forms best when you start to attend social events together that are outside of your work place. You quickly discover that you have more in common than just your career. You like hanging out with one another.

Volunteer events. I have talked to tons of people who give a significant amount of their time in volunteering in their community and for special charities and community events. From this, I have story after story of how the compassion they were showing the needy turned into a compassion or care for one other. They began to do lunch or outings and later became great friends.

Media. This is not to be underestimated. While many people meet up on social networks for the wrong reason, the meet and greet way of getting to know someone does not have to be a hazard. I simply encourage you not to allow the computer to be the divine between you and a potential friend. If there is to be something genuine and moral then by all means follow-up. Follow through on these types of connections in a safe place and in safe company. It is important to ascertain that you're not getting into something dangerous or life threatening. This platform can be a good connector if it is used properly and morally. In fact, it is really a great tool when used and not abused.

These are not the only ways, but I must say that I have seen it work almost one hundred percent of the time.

I have to share one last way you can meet friends. It is not original with me, it is straight out of the Bible.

Show yourself friendly. *"A man who wants friends must show himself friendly."* Proverb 18:24 You know, I am perplexed when I meet loners who say, "I have no friends." Uh, if you never ever try to make friends, the odds will be very high that you will not have friends. I repeat, Show Yourself Friendly!!! There are many people just like you who will welcome a solid, sincere friend if they knew the opportunity was possible. And the opportunity is possible!

In 1996 I was teaching at a very large ministry conference on the east coast of the United States. This conference was known for hosting a minimum of fifteen of the leading pastors and conference speakers annually — all in one week. And that did not include the front line musical guest of that day. They would come in from various parts of the United States and from all over the world.

My executive assistant at that time received a call from this ministry stating that I was being invited to teach at the conference for a main morning session. When she brought the news to me, I didn't believe it and thought she was playing a joke on me. We did that sometimes, as we would role play what the days ahead would look like for us, it was all an exercise in ever-increasing faith. She often said to me, "One day, you will be a guest at some of the larger conferences!" So, a lot of faith speaking and role playing was going on about this from time to time. We would even act out how she would respond to the call when she received it and how I would accept the call which would invite me to speak. My pre-rehearsed reaction to the said call that we were expecting to come in some day was always easy, "Yes, I accept!"

On this particular day, I thought she was joking about what we had been hoping for. When I learned it was a real call and not a joke, I was overcome with unbelief! She said, "You have been invited to speak just before Dr. Myles Monroe on a main morning session at the national conference in Maryland!" For those of you who might not be familiar with Dr. Monroe, he was a well-known Bahamian evangelist and ordained minister, as well as an author, speaker and leadership consultant who founded and led the Bahamas Faith Ministries International. A long story short, it was one of the most memorable invitations I'd ever accepted until this day! This was not just because I met Dr. Monroe but also because out of that one morning, I met two of the most amazing people who would go on to have both an inimitable and profound influence in my life. Most memorable!

Dr. Jacqueline M. Norris became a spiritual mom to me during the session. After hearing me speak she came up and said, "The Lord has told me to stay connected to you. You will be a blessing to my life and ministry and I plan to be a blessing to yours!" Oh was she ever right! We formed a real life mother-son bond as she become a spiritual parent in every sense of the word. I affectionately named her, 'Dr. Mom'. I spoke at her annual conferences. It was a divinely ordered friendship bond which lasted many years.

Dr. Mom was the epitome of someone who taught and walked out her faith — even in realms of supernatural faith. While I had a measure of the gift of faith working in my life, she added to it immensely over the years we walked together. When she transitioned to heaven, she made it clear to her board and succession team that the monthly support that her church was giving to my international efforts should continue.

Not long after her death, her successors, Pastors Barbara and Baron Brown became two of my spiritual mentees and great, great friends. They have allowed me to walk with them and the church at the highest levels of leadership. They are great pastors and great leaders! It is a pleasure to walk with and serve them. Out of this relationship with Dr. Mom, I got two more for the price of one!

Another notable friendship which comes to mind happened at a conference in which I spoke. I addressed the delegates in the morning session of the conference and come evening, I sat with my travel companions enjoying the evening speaker. During the meet and greet time, a certain gentleman, Ashley C. Estrada, approached me. He was attending the conference from St. Thomas in the Virgin Islands and was also a speaker in the lineup during the conference. He explained to me how the message from the morning service had been the most powerful one so far from his viewpoint. I knew he was being kind, because Dr. Myles Monroe, the "Purpose and Kingdom Man" had spoken after me. That says it all, yeah! I honestly did not think he was referring to me! He had been there from the start of the conference so I guess he felt he could make the claim safely. I thanked him for his kind remarks and as I turned to walk away, he said, "Would you mind if I gave you a gift?" I didn't know how to respond but it just seemed that "Yes" was an appropriate answer. This was all done in the open and those around us could hear him speaking to me. So, I said, 'Sure.' It was then that he gave me a ring and said, "You and I will be brothers in the gospel and the Lord will use us together to bless leaders. This will be a covenant of our brotherhood in Christ."

You can only imagine how shocked I was. This had never ever happened to me before. For a moment, I was speechless. I did not know what to say and I sure didn't know what to do with the ring. I refrained from becoming all weirded out in the moment. My mother had taught me to always say "Thank you" so I started there. It was a perfect fit too, so I wore the ring for the rest of the days I attended the conference.

Later after the evening worship, we met with the other guest pastors in the green room for fellowship. He came over and explained in more detail what the Lord was saying to him about the gift he gave me. He wanted me to understand what was going on and took time to explain how the ring was a sign of covenant friendship.

He proceeded to invite me to St. Thomas in the US Virgin Islands to be one of his frontline speakers at the next pastors and leaders conference that he held annually. What I did not know was the scope of how this conference attracted leaders from many of the Caribbean nations for one week every year. That one invitation opened so many of the Caribbean islands to me for ministry.

After teaching in his conference on the first day, while having lunch with his entourage including his family and some of his leaders, I clearly saw a friendship in the making. It was quick, it was godly. Today we are still brothers. He is changing the world through life-impacting care to people on several continents. We celebrate each other when we get a chance. He is a powerful leader with great influence for the Kingdom of God! Imagine how differently things would have turned out if I refused to accept his friendship or his token of friendship in the form of that ring. I write this to say that unusual circumstances can lead to great and godly friendships.

The close friendship with all four of these dear loved ones happened because they showed themselves friendly and I responded in like friendliness.

They all have been with me through some painful seasons of my life. When my mother passed, Barbara and Baron Brown drove eight hours one way and eight hours back to attend my mother's celebration of life. I didn't even know they were in the audience until the end of the service and as I was shaking hands and hugging people, there they stood in the receiving line. I nearly dropped to the floor. They both leaned over to me at the same time and warmly embraced me and said, "We just want you to know we love you and that we are here with and for you!" Afterwards, they got back into their car and drove back home.

Many other life giving friendships have come this same way. I am overwhelmingly blessed by my dear friends Randy and Callie Boyd who lead Prepare International in Lubbock, Texas. I met Randy while attending a gathering in the Mountains of North Carolina in 2012. After flying to Lubbock a month or so later I met Callie and their amazing children! Later, I met with the Prepare team. A bond was instantly formed. They allow me to serve with them in the discipleship of leaders in several nations of the world. Of the forty-four nations I've been to at the time of this writing, I have served in twelve nations for Prepare International. We do more than serve together; we do life together as family!

Friends! I call them the greatest gifts from the Lord to humanity!

Because of these friends, I received and continue to receive love, wisdom, counsel, support and care for me as a person. I have hurt safely in hurting times.

Sometimes, you have just got to show yourself vulnerable, and not hide yourself. Show yourself friendly!

By now, there should be some ideas and thoughts coming to your mind on how you will:

Select good friends

Spot sound and safe attributes

Sort your relationships for levels of sharing and caring

Switch a few people around who are in the wrong category of your life

And…

Show yourself friendly.

There is no reason to hurt alone — none whatsoever. There are many reasons to have friends come along and help you bear your burden and your hurts.

These Friends — true friends will not just pat your back and listen to you un-endlessly rehearse your hurts, the true friend will help you move on with your life!

FIVE
I Think I Hurt Myself — HELP!

Blame! It is one of the most natural and convenient things to do. You don't have to be taught to blame, it comes pre-packaged at birth. We start to do it from the moment we learn to speak. As you and I grew from infancy, to toddler, to adolescent to teenager to adults, we blamed. And the chances are no matter your present age you've blamed at least once in the past three days. Yes, it happens that frequently. For others of us it is more like a daily hobby so the blame-game happens more often. Of course that's not you! Or is it?

It feels right to say, "I did it" when something is going to work for our personal benefit. But, it also feels ok to say, "I didn't do it" when something is not going to work to our personal benefit — even if we did it. I didn't say that the latter was ok, I just said it often feels ok in the moment.

We also live in a society where blaming is fashionable. It is celebrated and embraced by the masses. It is nearly an addiction craze spinning out of control. You just have to listen to some of the American daytime TV talk shows!

Without blame, they would not have any guests to feature on those shows. In fact, in modern day society if you are not blaming then you are lame. You are not cool. My perspective is that all of this blaming is dumbing down our world. And when I say dumbing the world down, I'm saying it affects everyone from the highest offices in the land to our little innocent ones who haven't even had the fair chance to learn responsibility yet. Well, for what it is worth here are my thoughts: it is making us morally and emotionally sick and we have to stop all the blaming! Imagine if a law was passed that you could only speak positive things every day of your existence? Yes, I know, it is far-fetched, but imagine what would happen if the blame game stopped! People would actually have respect and caring for one another. My, how that would change society as a whole!

Try asking someone whether they did something bad or wrong today. They will first ask you, "What do you consider right" or "what is bad?" They will go on to say, "It is a matter of how you see it versus how I see it!" Then, they will immediately deny that they did anything at all. They will deny it with a straight face. I'm sorry but they will lie, keep a straight face and deny that they did anything wrong at all. If they should come close to owning up to being responsible for the wrong-doing they will follow up quickly with something like, "yes, the incident happened but it is/was not my fault."

In 2017, I was so touched by a time of fellowship that I had with an influential senior Pastor in another nation.

He wanted to talk over some real challenges in his life, ministry and even his marriage.

Moments after we got together for lunch, he immediately begin to speak candidly with me about what was going on. What was most surprising about this conversation was that only four minutes into listening to him, I was arrested by the fact that seven distinct times he made the statement "It is my fault!"

It grabbed my attention BIG TIME! I am a listener, I pay attention to details. When I hear something that is out the norm and redundant, I am on it. My ears and eyes are wide open. I am curious to learn how the repetitiveness connects with the issue being discussed.

Because I rarely hear someone taking the blame straight out of the gate, I briefly interrupted him — it's not my style to interrupt you know. I let people talk for at least fifty minutes before I will say one word. Sometimes, I will sense the need to let them talk beyond fifty minutes.

But this day I interrupted. I brought to his attention that he had owned up to the situations he found himself in and had done so seven times in four minutes. I wanted to know if he was aware of what he was doing and why he kept repeating the line, "It is my fault!"

So I asked him about this repetitiveness in admitting to being responsible. I thought maybe he was nervous or simply needed something to calm his nerves. He sounded like an MP3 tune on repeat.

He said to me, "I did not come to play with this matter. I came to get help for it. And I flew you in to get help. I don't wish to waste your time and so I thought it was important that you know I am to blame. I didn't come to make anyone else responsible for the mess I have made!"

What this good man was doing wasn't normal. Usually the norm is that most people give a bunch of explanations as to why something has gone bad and then will subtly admit they played a very, very small part in what is wrong — just about everybody sings the same tune with minimizing self-blame.

He was doing the exact opposite. He was owning the blame upfront and rather insistently instead of passing blame. Hardly anybody does that. He could have easily blamed others because of his esteemed position among leaders of the faith and his community, but he chose not to.

Ten minutes into my time with this good man, my respect level had risen to an all-time high. It had shot up to an 11 on a scale of 1-10. It was off the charts I tell you, off the charts! I already liked him, but that day, I loved him more. I saw him as a gentleman's, gentleman. He wasn't trying to play me or use me as a token to help him lie his way out of his mess. He was clearly done playing himself and anyone else for that matter. He wasn't using his position or popularity in the nation to get himself a free pass. He had hurt lots of people in his inner circle and he was also hurting. He wanted me to know that he was responsible and was ready to receive help.

One of the last lines he said in his forty minutes of talking was, "I know I have hurt myself and I need help." That day was so impactful to me. I was there to help, but I too was helped. I will never forget it. The Lord helped us both!

Much of our study so far in this book has focused upon issues and hurts that may be occurring in our lives because of something or someone else. And while I have briefly alluded to self-hurt, I have not given much time to it. I wish to give a little more time to it in this chapter.

Self-Hurt.

Studies show that a larger percentage of bad situations we get into are self-imposed or self-inflicted and can be prevented. In other words there are decisions and actions we can take to forego self-inflicted hurt. When we practice self-hurt, we walk into storms without umbrellas. When we don't take necessary steps, we will get rained upon and have to live with the results of our own poor choices.

I have observed this to be chronically true these days. Whether in our finances, health, relationships, or some other area, we make poor choices and allow things to go too far which leaves us hurt and disappointed. We quickly get into situations, but can't get out as quick as we got into them.

...Hmmmm, we get stuck.

For example... If you don't use a budget, but you spend, spend, spend, you will have financial issues. If you eat junk food all the time without eating healthy food or exercising you will have health issues. If you are unfaithful or unfair in your relationships, you will have relationship issues. If you abuse and misuse substances, you will predispose yourself to severe addictions, the loss of your family and loved ones, as well as to the possibility of various types of incurable diseases and possibly cancer.

You can't keep doing wrong stuff to yourself and then ask, "Why aren't things going right?"

It is fashionable to make something or someone else responsible for the messes that we make. But it is also foolishness. Sooner or later, blame will always turn the pointing finger back in the direction of the one who is really responsible. And even if you dodge and duck, it doesn't mean you are not being pointed at. Blame will blame you back!

It is important also to observe that there is a different outcome when we blame something versus blaming someone. We clearly as a society haven't figured this out yet. So, we just keep blaming everything and everybody.

Many hours during many sessions over many years as a pastoral counselor have been spent trying to get people to see that when we blame something such as culture, traffic, the weather, politics and even the dog for what went wrong, while it is wrong to pass the blame, it is not quite the same as when we blame people for our shortcomings.

If you blame the culture, traffic, weather, politics or the dog, tomorrow things will go on as usual and there will be no real major fall outs. Culture will be culture, traffic will be traffic, weather is weather, politics will still be politics and the dog will be the dog.

On the other hand when we blame people for our shortcomings, we inflict hurt, pain and bitterness in our relationships. We damage one another. When you and I start to carelessly tear into our relationships, we slowly lose them. No matter how you size it up, the loss of relationships is huge in proportion to things. Those we blame and tear into results in a broken, difficult and sometimes irreparable relationship. Relationships are left bruised and broken and very often the person blamed is left broken and destroyed. We break their love, faith, and trust in us. This is far more serious.

Most of society does not really understand the long-term consequence we will pay if we continue to morph into a blaming society. The price we are paying right now is the loss of decency required to live together as a society in love, honesty, trust, community and peace. Neighbors are no longer people you can trust, nor want to trust because the decency and the moral compass of our neighbors have often gone south. I am not saying that all neighbors are morally corrupt, but if you just look at the news and the noise on social media, brother betrays brother, and if you can get ahead at the cost of using someone, that too is celebrated. We are losing. If we don't stop blaming and own up to our responsibility the debt will be much too big to pay and the damage too major to repair.

As I finished listening to the pastor I mentioned earlier, I saw his literal countenance change by the end of our fellowship — he was glowing! Admittedly it was one of the most welcoming fellowships I'd ever been a part of. It didn't have to explode before I could help him. It was so easy to provide help in this encounter!

He has been on the mend and the Lord has restored him because he said, "I am to blame, it is my fault!" Hallelujah!

That day was really amazing in more ways than one. He got the help he needed. I was blessed and learned from him. He paid for the meal that we had at a five star restaurant. In fact, while we ate he was pointing out to me the various governmental, business and public dignitaries of his nation that were sitting all around us. Many of them he knew on a first name basis. They stopped by the table one-by-one to chat. What a day! I bring this point up only to share that fame and connections do not preclude us from hurting ourselves or others. We all need help and so often a type of deliverance from ourselves, especially when we are in a position of power!

Ok, you know what is coming now... I have to ask you about your hurt.

Is it self-inflicted; did you bring it upon yourself?

The question is not to accuse you, point a finger at you or blame you for what is happening. I am not trying to catch you in something. You may already be caught so you don't need me or anyone to catch you in something. I merely ask so we can determine what or who is causing the hurt.

If it is you, we must address it in the same forward manner we addressed hurts in the previous chapters. If you are responsible for your own hurt but you start your explanation with, "I did not do it or it isn't my fault," when then you will greatly slim your chances for getting unstuck.

My sweet late mother, Helen Marie Boston, when she'd catch me in something as a child would say, "Walter Jr., you may be getting by, but you are not getting away. It will catch up with after a while son, if you don't stop!"

If you don't confront the issues that you are causing they will confront you. When they do, they will confront you face on with all of their fury. This is usually a slow cycle of personal and public humiliation that can be avoided.

Why do we avoid owning our self-inflicted hurt and blame others so easily and quickly? Here are the top reasons as I see them.

Shame. We blame so we won't be shamed. We don't want to be shamed before everyone. We don't want our name or reputation destroyed. We don't wish to lose our position and popularity. That list goes on and on. So we blame to avoid the shame that might come in that moment. We talk ourselves into believing that it will go away and that things will be just fine. Do you have a few stories on how that has not worked? Are you are still trying to clean up the trash left behind from the last blame game? I am telling you blame games are nearly impossible to win.

Selfishness. At the heart of why we blame others is because we are looking out for ourselves. There is something very pathetic about not caring how we hurt or how much we hurt others. A selfish person has no feelings about the hurt they cause. They are cold in their souls. Selfishness is one of the ugliest spirits I have ever encountered. It does not care about anyone or anything except self. It will blame and never ever consider the horrible consequences it causes others. Selfish people will see the harm they have caused and still not care at all.

Stupidity. For some reason we are willing to gamble our common sense and dumb down our sound judgment. We know better but we just don't do better. So we fall into stupidity. We play the role of a fool and the whole time we are the one being fooled. The end result is not only do we behave stupidly but we come out looking stupid.

Strong headedness. When someone is strong headed they don't listen. When you don't listen you will crash soon because you are determined to have it your way no matter what about most things (if not everything). A strong-headed person will have a rough road to travel in life. The road is filled with lots of hurt, pain and detachment. They often also make it painful for those closest to them.

Sin. This is how we get stuck in the first place. We believe we can commit sins and because they are committed in private we can keep committing them privately without any consequences. Maybe you never set out to believe this and behave this way, but the problem with this belief is that you did not get the memo that warns: *sin talks and it has a big mouth!* You see sin will put you on blast. It beams above your head in imaginary neon lights. It will reveal even that which you thought was your ultra-private stuff. Don't believe the lie that it is your private life. Sin will prove you wrong every single time. Before you know it, your sin will be the headlines of your public life.

I take self-inventory very often — sometimes daily — to make sure the points above are not controlling my life. I admit sometimes, they get in but I have vowed not to let them take up permanent residence. I invite you to do the same.

Help me stop hurting myself.

It has been said, *"The world will come at you with knives so you don't need to cut yourself."*

We live in a time when so much negativity is so readily available. If you are not careful you will be bleeding from its impact and it will take a while to realize that you have been cut and are bleeding. And, the worst part is that nobody else was involved, you did it!

We must avoid cutting ourselves. We must avoid it at all cost. If it does happen or has happened by whatever means, then we must address the bleeding no matter who is responsible for the hurt.

In graduate school I took two introductory psychology courses on the subject. From these classes I had to write several papers in order to fulfill the course requirements and one of my papers addressed how to stop hurting.

I love acrostics so I decided to write the paper on the word S.T.O.P. I was hoping to create a path on how to conquer hurt, harm and other related defeating pathologies. I believe conquering is better than coping with hurt. I will share my acrostic with you. I have used it for years to get people moving in the right direction to escape all kinds of hurt.

For this book I replaced all of the verbiage I used in my research paper with layman's everybody, everyday language because my dissertation was research and required an academic approach. That is not needed here.

Let's go for it!

S. T. O. P.

S. *Speak up about how you are hurting yourself.* Like the pastor in the beginning of this chapter if you don't speak up you won't be heard. You will hide and never heal. Just like one friend said to me years ago, "Walter, you need to tattle to someone trustworthy about yourself just like you would tell on someone else if you witnessed them harming themselves." He would shout, "Tell it! And tell it all!" I still laugh when I hear his voice saying that. And it is true.

T. *Take a step or a leap for help.* When you have been in a place of hurt for so long you lose hope for just about everything else. At some point you will have to take baby steps towards help. By this I mean, maybe you can't share everything all at once. And maybe you shouldn't. But, share a little at a time with the right person. Whether the leap encompasses baby steps or a leap of giant steps, you can't stay where you are. You will lose the battle. Close your eyes and step or leap in to help!

Override negative thoughts. Negative thoughts like blame, guilt, hopelessness and more will press on you. There will be many times you'll have to do what I called, a 'brain override.' In the world of technology IT specialists fix computers that have been attacked by a virus by performing an override to restore the computer to its operating system. The brain works very similarly. Do an override every day if you have to until your system starts to think new thoughts instead of old thoughts; positive thoughts over negative thoughts.

Pray for guidance. Ask the Lord for guidance. There are some victories you will not accomplish alone no matter how strong you are. You will need help beyond yourself and beyond this world. Overcoming self-hurt is a process like any other type of hurt; you will need guidance. The Lord will not only guide you. He will guide you with His eyes on you. In other words, He will watch out for you until you get where you are going. He will help you end up on the right path of life and victory.

A deeper discussion for a deeper matter

Briefly, I want to address two final thoughts before closing this chapter. The first is what self-inflicted hurt sometimes leads to if not properly addressed and resolved.

First. Self-Harm

Self-harm is different than self-hurt. It is when you turn your emotional hurt into physical hurt causing personal bodily injury to yourself. Self-harm is cutting, bruising or inflicting harm to your body to the point of bleeding. This sort of personal abuse is very serious, dangerous and life threatening. It has an occurrence which is far too high among many — both young and old, male and female alike. Non-Suicidal-Self-Injury (NSSI) is appearing on scene in far more numbers, but it is a hush topic not talked about. If you, or someone you know is dealing with their personal hurt in this way, you must seek help immediately. In fact, stop reading this book, get your phone and call for help immediately. I recommend you speak with your physician who can refer you to the proper help. If you don't have a physician speak to your spiritual leader or someone who has access to a pool of professionals that can care for you.

A few facts.

Self-harm appears in high numbers among teenagers. Some numbers support up to 70% in our society practice this destructive behavior. I personally think the numbers are much higher. This behavior often follows teens into their adult life.

Self-harm is a familiar but false go-to method to cope with deep-seated hurt, anger, pain and even emotional and physical abuse that has happened. It is blaming yourself and punishing yourself physically.

Self-harm shows up in all groups of people. So don't buy into the lie that it only happens to you or a select few. That is the lie we often hear in our head. To feel this way will make you silent about something that you really need to be vocal about.

Second. An evil spirit or demonic problem

As a pastor, I have to address the truth that sometimes hurts and iniquities go far beyond someone being offended, disappointed, hurt and let down. It is not just emotional and mental but quite often it is spiritual. I have seen my share of situations where hurt was spiritual and there was a need for deliverance. By deliverance I mean help from the Lord through prayer to overcome an evil spirit inciting the pain on many levels in someone's life.

Let me explain what I mean by this.

I recognize that some of the readers of this book may not be people of faith and therefore I do not want to lose anyone in my attempt to be clear on this subject.

There are times when unaddressed hurt is allowed to linger for months, years, and even generations. They become unrelenting and agitating curses eating away at the core of our souls. This may often show up initially as anger, unforgiveness, jealousy, bitterness and a host of other negative emotions. When unaddressed for extended periods of time these emotions can take on a life of their own and are driven and controlled by evil spirits.

The spirit world is a world that we cannot see, but we can be influenced by it. It is as real as the world we live in and see. Both good and evil co-exist in the spirit world. Generally when we speak of the good, we refer to God or even the Holy Spirit. According to the Scriptures, we are compassed about by the presence of angels in our lives; imagine that… angels working in and for us. This is true. I have a few stories to tell you! I know… another book!

Therefore when the influence is bad or dark, it is the work of evil spirits or demons. Their main goal is to destroy us by any means at their disposal. They don't care how, they will even use you as the weapon to take yourself out.

If fact, I believe that self-harm is a clear sign that self-hurt has gone to the place of demonic influence and the dark work of evil spirits in most people battling this affliction. I'll support my belief in just a moment. Hold tight!

When people start to cut and hurt themselves they feel compelled beyond themselves to inflict the harm and usually hear voices and feel urges that are not human or normal. They are pushed and sometimes driven to hurt themselves. Sometimes they are even driven to hurt others.

Last year while preaching in the state of Virginia, the host pastor told me of a young mother who was being charged with murder and a host of other crimes she committed on her infant child. It was reported that she had been emotionally and mentally hurting from a personal intimate relationship gone bad between her and another man. She could not get beyond the pain. So, she began to cut herself. When it was discovered, caring individuals involved in her life sought to get her help. One day while alone, she lost it mentally and emotionally and ended up putting her young baby into a kitchen oven and cooking the infant alive.

Let me tell you again, self-harm is a serious and urgent matter. Clearly this mother's actions were driven by demonic influence. Evil spirits were at work in her whether you believe in them or not. That is not human behavior! It is not the behavior of a mother towards her child. It is something only an evil spirit will drive someone to do. There is no other sane explanation.

When we see behavior at this level there is an urgent need for someone who can help you be delivered from demonic influence or evil spirits.

In the Bible, Mark 5:1-15 recounts a story of a man who was in the clutches of demons and trapped by the habit of inflicting self-harm. The only way he could get delivered from the entities controlling him was to have the evil spirits that were causing self-harm cast out of him by godly personas who knew what they were doing! Jesus was that godly persona!

I asked you earlier to hold tight because I would later support my belief in demonic spirits and their destructive influences upon our lives.

Let's have a look in the scriptures at what is said about this man:

"They arrived in the territory of the Gerasenes on the other side of the Sea of Galilee. As Jesus stepped out of the boat, a man came out of the tombs and met him. The man was controlled by an evil spirit and lived among the tombs. No one could restrain him any longer, not even with a chain. He had often been chained hand and foot. However, he snapped the chains from his hands and broke the chains from his feet. No one could control him. (He was not Hercules) Night and day he was among the tombs and on the mountainsides screaming and cutting himself with stones. The man saw Jesus at a distance. So he ran lto Jesusl, bowed down in front of him, and shouted, "Why are you bothering me now, Jesus, Son of the Most High God? Swear to God that you won't torture me." He shouted this because Jesus said, "You evil spirit, come out of the man." Jesus asked him, "What is your name?" He told Jesus, "My name is Legion [Six Thousand], because there are many of us." He begged Jesus not to send them out of the territory. A large herd of pigs was feeding on a mountainside nearby. The demons begged him, "Send us into the pigs! Let us enter them!" Jesus let them do this. The evil spirits came out of the man and went into the pigs. The herd of about two thousand pigs rushed down the cliff into the sea and drowned. Those who took care of the pigs ran away. In the city and countryside they reported everything that had happened. So the people came to see what had happened. They came to Jesus and saw the man who had been possessed by the legion of demons. The man was sitting there dressed and in his right mind."

I will not teach point by point on this passage although I am so tempted to do so. Hey, I am a pastor, and this lesson will preach or teach — whichever you prefer. I'm holding myself back… I am not going to do either one!

Seriously, I want to have us look at some of the major behaviors highlighted in this man possessed by evil spirits. To see them gives us a clear look into how to identify the difference between someone that is hurting because they hurt themselves through poor choices, versus someone who is trapped in self-harm, meaning they are physically harming themselves, with brute strength I might add.

The self-hurting man who harmed himself…

- Lived among the tombs. This means he preferred to be among the dead instead of the living. *This is the hiding and isolation I've been teaching you about throughout the book. This is it at an ultimate level of pain that is self-destructive.*
- Was controlled by evil spirits. This means he had lost personal control and the spirits took over. *I have talked in the book about those moments when you feel clueless or without control to help yourself.*
- Was chained or in chains and still could not be restrained. *This is something far deeper than hurt feelings or emotions when you are out of control physically. It is being stuck at a spirit level an evil spirit level. It is control gone out of control.*
- *Cut himself night and day and would be screaming. *This is not just self-hurt, this is self-harm. It is inflicting personal injury to yourself until it causes agony that is expressed vocally.*
- Was not just under the influence of one evil spirit, but many. The evil spirits identified themselves by the name "Legion" which means many! We are told in the text that there were six thousand evil spirits torturing this man. *You see why I am saying this is a deeper kind of hurt that can cause a deeper kind of pain that needs intervention beyond science, medicine and talking to someone. It needs prayer and the power*

> *of the Holy Spirit who can address the evil spirit calling or casting it out.*

- Was often without his clothes. *This was not because he was having panic attacks or was too hot, or a nudist at heart or was close to the beach in the summer. This was the influence of the evil spirits working on him.*

When the evil spirits were cast out of the man by Jesus, we find him sitting and dressed and in his right mind.

I must interject here, if you feel lately that you have been dealing with something deeper than just self-hurt or embarrassment, and you have been having thoughts of personal harm, you need to talk with a pastor, priest, or some reputable spiritual leader who can get you help for the deeper issue at play in your life. Evil spirits are not playing with you, they are out to harm you and possibly kill you.

You will know that you have been freed when you, like the man in Mark 5, can sit and be clothed in your right mind.

I fully recognize that we have taken several sharp turns since starting this chapter. Unlike the other chapters it has opened up deeper conversation and perhaps has stirred deeper wells.

I want you free — unstuck. That is why I wrote this book! So we have arrived at the destination — the stuff we have to talk about.

If you think — even for a split second — that the hurt that is going on in your life is self-imposed hurt, self-harm or even evil spirits, PLEASE… today, right now, I am asking you, I am begging you… take the next step and use your cell phone to call for help and save your life!

In previous chapters I have assured you that help is available. In this chapter I assure you again, real help is available!

You can get unstuck and MOVE ON!

SIX
If You Are Not
Moving You Are Stuck

Open any internet browser and search for men and women who have had to overcome pain, difficulty and failure and the list of biographies will wow you! You would not have paper enough in your printer to print out the list, in fact you might destroy a forest to supply the paper needed!

Within the pages of the Bible, you will see the same pattern. You may be familiar with the Bible stories of your youth where David was able to slay Goliath, and Jonah got out of the belly of the whale, but aside from these great accounts of the power of God, I am here to tell you that the Holy Book as it has been called is a wonderful amalgamation of stories showing the frailties and the fall-out of the ones who walked with God or who chose their own means to over following in His ways. Take a read through the Bible and you will see the exact same pattern as what a Google search might produce: people who went through levels of deep pain, hurt and loss.

What about a walk down memory lane in your life? You have stories of pain and failure you had to endure to stay in the game of life. It isn't always fun, most of the time it is hard, with little glimpses of happiness and joy within the screenplay. It is never a feel-good Hollywood flick where everything turns out and the guy gets the girl, they have 2.3 children, a wonderful dog and a house in the suburbs, oh and let's not forget the fancy cars as well as money, money, money!

The pain, failure and disappointments are things we all have in common. What each of us share in common is that we had to let go so that the future could happen. We simply cannot stay in the same place and move forward at the same time. It is like quicksand if we try to do so. The more you struggle to stay there, the deeper you sink until such time the sands overcome you and choke the life out of you.

I think often about my days growing up in my home city and neighborhood community! In fact, there are many times I recall a memory with a grin, laughter and a thrill of joy. I guess you could say they were good old days.

When I think of them, I can often see the park I played in across from my grandmother's house in my mind's eye. It was my little piece of heaven as a kid. The two places I loved the most apart from home was being in church and at the park — in that order.

The park was a little piece of heaven for all the community kids. I am not exaggerating when I tell you the park was the size of a small community block. It had all the standard play gear — swings, monkey bars, sliding boards, seesaws, merry go rounds — and extra amenities such as a horse shoe area, two basketball courts, a tennis court, volleyball area, a baseball field that lit up at night and more. Oh, and did I mention it had two sheltered picnic table areas where you could eat and play cards, board games and more. When the sun was too blistering to play on the grass, or when the summer showers came, the sheltered area made it perfect to continue playing under cover. During the summer time we even had free lunch programs that were sponsored by the city. Every child who wanted to partake could come to the park for a free bagged lunch! The summer program also had so many other opportunities built into it like field trips and more. To top it off the park bore the name of the famous African American baseball player, Buck Lenard. It was a real community park!

Beside the park most of the neighborhood kids had their own backyards that had a variety of fruit and nut trees and some berry vines, and some even had their own mini gardens. The backyards were large enough to play a good game of hide and seek or kickball without breaking a car or house window. It was really nice because those were the days when children played outside. There were no cell phones, internet, gaming devices, YouTube or Netflix; in fact, there were no fax machines! So playing outside was the thing. On Saturday mornings, you would stay in to watch cartoons at least until 11 or 12 noon. And on Sundays most families went to church. We had several community churches that were all within walking distance. So you could choose your "brand of Sunday morning worship."

We also had three different neighborhood stores who all sold many flavors of ice cream by the scoop and many varieties of cookies and candies to choose from. These were the days of three for a penny candies. A whole bagful could be purchased for a nickel. An ice cream was 5 cents or thereabouts, and usually it melted faster than you could eat the voluminous amount of your favorite ice cream sitting in a cone. Listen, those three stores were the throne room of the Lord in my child's mind. Of course, I'm just kidding! But in reality for every kid they were one of the highlight of the community. This was especially true at allowance time, or after acquiring some spare money from doing community yard work for a neighbor or when a good ole uncle came around who had money.

Hey, I told you the place was like a little heaven, especially for us young'uns.

Please don't read this wrong, our neighborhood was not comprised of the big brick houses, manicured lawns or big cars. All of that was just across the highway on the other side. When we wanted to see those things, we'd just cross over the main city street that separated the neighborhoods and walk around while we would "oooh and ahhhh" about how one day we'd get a nice, big home and car like what we were seeing on the other side of the highway.

Nostalgic memories of my early years in that community fell into my thoughts and lingered there for a season a few years back. In that time-frame, I decided while returning from one of my road trips involving service in several cities that I would drive through my hometown on the way back home to Charlotte, North Carolina. I had not been in Rocky Mount, North Carolina — not to be confused with the Rocky Mountains — in a long while. I was itching to see my childhood kingdom again and was hoping it would bring back even more vivid, happy memories. And so I commanded my car's navigation to put in the address to my old place at 516 Henry Street, Rocky Mount, North Carolina, and I started driving in that direction smiling like a fella who had just won a couple million dollars. I had my I-Phone ready for pictures and videos. I was READY!

A few hours later, upon reaching the community, I entered it near the park where I had grown up. The park was one of the main entry points into the "Little Raleigh Community" The horrors I saw that day did not register with what I was looking for or what I had remembered. It was as if I entered an entirely different community and one that was far, far removed from what I had grown up in.

The place was all run down and the more I drove into the community the more my heart broke with unbelief and dismay. It was as though a nuclear fallout had happened compared to the idyllic memories of my childhood. As I continued to drive, I even found myself starting to sniffle and release tears because of the gross deterioration I was seeing.

The park had many missing features. The fenced in baseball field with its side bleachers were gone; the tennis court was gone; the several big shade tree with the park benches for relaxing were gone; the basketball court was still there but only two old rusted out goals and rims without nets remained, and the marked concrete slab was cracking so bad you couldn't play any games on it. The picnic shelters were gone; there was no hint that there was ever a horse shoe or volley ball area and the swings and other park gear were in a deplorable condition. It bore no hint of the idyllic yesteryear of my childhood. It truly resembled an area ravaged by war and destruction.

As I continued to drive through the community many of the homes that surrounded the park were in dilapidation or no longer there. The streets of the community were filthy and houses were boarded up — they were eyesores in every sense of the word and needed to be torn down.

I decided to drive onward to see about the three community stores that we patronized — especially in the summer — to get ice cream, soda and snacks. All three stores were not only out of business, they were boarded up and overgrown by weeds and bushes. My heart by this time felt like it was very close to having a mild cardiac arrest in need of defibrillation — a shock or three!

The community was layered in city blocks so navigating it was very easy. You just went from one street to another and you would still be in the community.

I saved my beloved Henry Street for last. Now that I think back our neighborhood streets all had the names of people: Henry, Clyde, Lindsay, Lane, Dexter, Luper, and on and on they went. Our community didn't have any drives, circles, lanes, boulevards or cul-de-sacs, just streets. On the other side of the main road in the other neighborhood where the manicured lawns and the big cars were parked, if you were fortunate enough you could live on a Drive, Lane, Circle or Boulevard.

When I turned on Henry Street, I thought I had turned into a city dump. House after house along my beloved street showed the signs of abandonment where once-vibrant homes were now boarded up and empty spaces where houses once stood were overgrown with weeds and brush of the prickly variety. I half imagined Tarzan would come swinging through the trees. The place was filthy with litter. For a moment I stopped the car and pulled over to the curb to double check if I'd driven into the wrong community. Just maybe I was off slightly and didn't realize it. After all I had been driving for a while by this time, nearly four hours. But I was not in a wrong location I was in the right community.

My old memories and my current thoughts were clashing. I had expected that after many years it would not be the same, but I had hoped and even imagined it would at least be improved and modernized. It was neither. It was everything but modernized.

When I drove up to my childhood home I almost passed by it. Not because I didn't remember where I lived, I will never forgot my childhood home. It really was a home and not just a house. I nearly passed it because it was no longer visible from the street. It was still standing, but barely. It was falling down, and the roof was collapsed. The windows were all broken out, the place was boarded up and it was also overgrown by weeds and bushes. You could hardly see the structure. It looked like someone had dropped a bomb on my childhood home. And that's putting it mildly. My emotions for a moment went in several different directions.

That is when I lost it. In my parked car, I broke into tears. I tried to figure out what had gone wrong. What happened to "Little Raleigh?" What happened to my childhood home?

The good old sites that afforded me my wonderful childhood days were all gone. There was a desperate need for some good new days to come to the neighborhood!

Several things were very clear.

Progress had come to a complete halt.

Life had stopped moving forward. It wasn't even standing still. It seemingly regressed to an ugliness that is not describable.

The place was not only stuck in the past but had fallen back in its appearance. There no longer was any semblance of what it was at its pinnacle with Saturdays in the park with children laughing, playing, picnics, fresh air, ice cream and activities. Not an iota of any happiness remained, not even enough to have warm memories of the place. It was ghetto in its worst form. People obviously quit caring about the area and Little Raleigh in its quaintness was no more.

I thought to myself what happened to my childhood neighborhood is common and eerily similar and familiar to our lives.

In fact it is common to hear people reference how their lives used to be. They go on to tell of their past which included beauty, progress, happiness, and passion. It doesn't matter if it was "poor" by some people's standards, it is what they remember and it was rightly so. Then after an unfortunate encounter with failure, disappointment and hurt, or failing to care and care-take, their lives pause and often come to a complete standstill. Some even go backward like my community had done. Spiritual, physical, mental, emotional and personal development all cease, leaving the inhabitants with broken memories of what it used to be like. The sad reality is they will speak of the past like it is the present.

In light of the good progress that you and I have made through the chapters of this book, this chapter is dedicated to making sure that we don't just move in a hot-foot on one spot dance pattern, trying to avoid imminent pain in the moment, but that we keep moving forward step by step and stride by stride.

Together, let's identify and explore some ways to avoid becoming a wasteland like the community you just read about. You have put in great sacrifice of time and effort to read up to this point. Along the way you have been making tough decisions to get unstuck. We must keep going and growing.

So let me ask you:

Do you have a mindset to keep moving?

Do you still have hope?

Do you have an intolerance for apathy?

Do you have a hunger for change?

Your honest answers to these questions determines the "Next" for the rest of your life.

The reality is if something is not moving it is standing still if it is standing still it is not changing and; if it is not changing it is dying.

This will not be you. You have come too far to stagnate or die.

I want to make sure that your pattern of thoughts and behaviors will not sabotage consistent movement in your life.

To do this I will share with you my so-called "Destructive Behavioral Syndromes" (DBS). These are concepts I developed and put to paper thirty-two years ago when the yellow legal pad and a roller ball pen was the number one way to make notes. I observed that we practice my DBS's frequently not even realizing that we are doing so. I saw them then and see them now as common behaviors in everyone.

I have given these behaviors a name and brief description to identify and define them. They are simple, consistent behaviors which will either help or hinder us.

Let's go…!

Personal perception syndrome. This is when attitude determines personal viewpoint. How you see everything about your existence determines how you speak and how you speak communicates how you stand by your personal views.

For a short while in the beginning of my pastoral leadership, I was perplexed at how the same conversation on the same subject was viewed many different ways. When this happens there is tendency to want to argue about who is right and who is wrong. After a while this approach only complicated my counseling sessions, board meetings, staff meeting and even some of my relationships. I soon came to learn and value the equal importance on how a topic is viewed and the attitude behind a personal viewpoint. Another epiphany happened one day around the one year mark into my pastoral position. The light bulb went on and all of a sudden I now realized that all of us speak passionately about topics based upon how we perceive them.

For example leaders see and speak differently than followers; politicians see and speak differently than the citizens; educators speak and see differently than students; business leaders see and speak differently than consumers, women see and speak differently than men; teenagers see and speak very differently than their parents — all on the same subjects Even the generation you belong to makes your viewpoints differ from that of the next generation. The goal should not be to pit one group against the other about who is right or wrong, but to see the viewpoints in a fashion to garner unity and forward movement. Prideful ego will always sink our efforts like the Titanic, the ship touted as "unsinkable" before she collided with an iceberg on April 14, 1912 and you know the rest of the story.

Our perception is born out of our perspective, and we stand by "how we see" no matter who else doesn't see it. A willingness to see something the way someone else does or doesn't mean you have to agree with their viewpoint, it just means you have agreed to see the other person's viewpoint. If you just try to see the other person's view before slaying or opposing it, it will move a conversation from the "stuck" mode to progressing. If you refuse to see the other person's viewpoint, it will usually keep the conversation in stuck mode and perhaps the conversation will never happen again.

Active action or reactive syndrome. This is when non-verbal communication shouts with a louder voice or actions than anything audible and a single word is never spoken.

Think of the many times you got stuck on how someone looked at you, gestured towards you or they were rudely dismissive by their posture. When it happened you didn't hear anything as nothing audible was spoken. This behavior determines ninety percent of the where, the how and the when of things moving on. One action or reactive move will sound out like a megaphone surpassing one thousand clearly spoken words every single time.

For example, if you ask someone if they would like to ride with you to the store and they reply, "Sure" but, immediately afterwards they sigh and slump into a "not really" posture you are hearing very loud words in your head by their non-verbal cue. What happened? You received two opposing answers in one reply. The verbal answer you heard was "Yes." The sigh and posture you saw was the action or reaction that said, "No, I really don't want to go with you!" The non-verbal was louder than the verbal. Now you don't want them to go with you... and you think to yourself, "Just stay where you are then" and all because of their action, they get your mental reaction and they clearly read your body language! Isn't it funny how so much can be spoken in silence? Perceptive? Yes!

Positional Judgment syndrome. This is when you make assumptions and personal opinions without regard for the truth. You take a position and present it as fact before it is proven factual.

This is the quickest way to offend one another. It immediately always stirs up negative emotions. When people are offended they back off, they stop coming around, they stop calling, texting or talking. They no longer desire to move forward with you and therefore, they move as far away from you as they can.

There are many challenges with this syndrome.

For one, it causes deep hurt and alienation. It will keep people on "stuck" mode generation after generation.

Two, this syndrome attacks the values and character of a person. When we attack each other in this way, this is very little forward movement.

Hasty Impulse Syndrome. This is when things have to be done right away with no consequential thought given to the outcome. A compulsion becomes a jail cell hard to break free from.

This behavior is driven by anxiousness and lingering thoughts that persist until they push you into something sordid and not above-board before you know it.

You only have to look at a purchase that you made, but now you regret it; a relationship you are in, but now you regret it; or a pizza you ate because your taste buds had to have it, but now you regret it. In fact you had to have two or three pizzas all in one week, or maybe one night! Your tummy hurts and your carbohydrate allotment has hit an all-time high, and your pants are a little tight.

This syndrome has stopped a lot of forward movement in its tracks. It has a swift bite but requires long-term recovery. It also plays with your thoughts until you feel like you are going crazy in your head. You have to learn to shut your "self-talker" off in your head if you refuse to be pushed around by this syndrome.

Everyday Routine Syndrome. This is when you get stuck in the day-to-day routine until it becomes your custom, your norm. There is no change or progress and there hasn't been in years. You settle in, perhaps thankful for the rut of complacency and before you know it things start to fall down.

This is what happened to my childhood community. The place was thriving when I was a child living there. Somewhere along the way, it got stuck in the day-to-day until the day-to-day became the norm where people settled down, and eventually the settling down lead to it falling down.

This also happens in our personal lives. We get to the new place and we like it, in fact, we fall in love with it. We wouldn't dream of having it any other way. So, we settle down and we overstay in the new place until it becomes the old place.

For a combination of reasons we lose momentum to stay current or relevant. We start to make statements like, "This is the way it has always been and it still works so why change anything?"

This is a suicidal syndrome. It thrives on apathy.

In our world everything is rapidly changing. If you don't keep up you will be left behind. The world around us is changing faster than we wish it to. Stay where you are and do nothing new to change and keep up and you will become irrelevant.

Let me illustrate.

What if in 2019 you consulted with a surgeon who was a leading physician in the decade of the 1970s? During that time he had a ubiquitous reputation as an awarding winning surgeon. It is now 2019 and he still performs surgeries on occasion but mainly practices general family medicine. As time has passed, he has not remained current with new medical technologies, developments and advancements.

One day you become very ill and learn that you will need surgery to mend. The good ole doctor from the 70's has space on his books to see you. You make an appointment and visit his office. After his examination, he diagnoses your condition as a form of cancer and offers to perform your surgery. He says to you, "I have not kept up with the updates in treating your type of cancer because modern medicine is too complicated. I don't know much about it at all, but cancer is cancer. I know you are aware of my success as a surgeon in the 70's on other types of cancers. So I look forward to doing your surgery and I hope the procedure will come out fine. I haven't done this procedure before but all surgeries are mostly the same. You just go in and cut it out and wait for recovery."

What the surgeon doesn't acknowledge is that your type of cancer can be cured non-invasively. New medicines and treatments can cure it in just ten visits over ten months at the cancer treatment center in your city. But the well-known surgeon from the 70's is talking about invasive surgery.

You bring to his attention that you have had several family members and friends who have had the same type of cancer and were cured without being cut open. He replies, "Oh, I bet they used one of those new young doctors. Those guys are not helping people, they are killing them. They need to learn the old way of doing things. That is the best way!"

Let me ask you, would you look for another doctor?

Of course! You would not allow the doctor who is stuck in routine — no matter how good he was years ago — do surgery on you using outdated procedures and practices. You would not have it, not now, not later!

You would thank him for his time and run out of his office so fast you risk getting a speeding ticket at the rate you are sprinting away. Yes, I'm joking but you get my point!

So it is with life. If you are going to keep moving you have got to stay current and avoid everyday routine syndrome. If you don't, several things will be obvious very quickly.

You will be stuck while thinking you are ok.

You will think everybody else is moving too fast and that they need to slow down and do things the old fashioned way, i.e. "The good old way!" Just think, if we all thought this way, we would all be riding horses, and lighting our houses with candles! Indoor plumbing would not be a part of the modern luxuries we get to enjoy. I think you get my point!!!

You will be stuck in loving the good old days — which I might add are never as good as we think they are — and miss out on the good new days.

You will be left behind and will blame others for not including you

You will try to live in the new world using old antiquated techniques that no longer apply or function.

Let me illustrate.

It would be like having a flip phone that still makes calls and maybe even allows you to text but in the present day I-Phones and Smartphones are in vogue. You may love your flip-phone, but the day you observe someone with a fancy phone that they can make calls, text, read books, shop online, control their car, home and a few other devices from, your phone ceases to be relevant when you compare the two. So you ask them, "Do you think I can do that on my phone? I don't like them new phones, and I just prefer keeping my flip phone. I have had it for fifteen years and it is paid for and nothing is wrong with it."

The person with the flip phone is right in his or her conclusion. There is nothing wrong with the flip phone and it is paid for, but there is something wrong with their way of thinking if they think themselves able to get all of the new technology on a dinosaur flip phone with outdated technology.

Until they change their mindset their world will continue to move at a snail's pace. One day they will try to make a simple phone call or text using the flip-phone and it will not serve them because it will no longer be compatible with any new cellular or satellite technology.

Don't get stuck. And never use age as an excuse. It usually sounds like this, "Dem young folks, versus us old folks!" Please don't ever get stuck! PLEASE!

Not long ago I stopped to have lunch at a Chic-Fil-A. This is a very popular fast-food restaurant in the United States.

They are known for good chicken sandwiches, waffles fries and great customer service. Their menu carries some other pretty good options too! When you go to their restaurants, they often have greeters who will serve you at your table by topping off your drinks, getting you more condiments if you need them and disposing of your food tray when you are done eating. The greeters are mostly senior citizens, but some restaurants have young greeters as well. The young crowd are usually cashiers inside the restaurant who man the drive through cash register and who fill the orders at the counter. On this day, when I walked into the restaurant, I was helped by a lady who appeared to be in her late 60's at a glance. I thought, 'Hmm, this is different. Maybe she is just calling me up and then one of the kids will take my order.'

Well, I was wrong, wrong, wrong!

I went up to the counter and she asked, "How may I help you today?" She proceeded to take my order. She did it fast, proficiently with a big smile on her face and she had me set up in a flash. I noticed two things. One, she never got the order wrong, and that was key because I changed my market salad to ordering grilled chicken nuggets instead of the grilled sliced chicken that comes pre made on it. This also insures I get the salad made fresh instead of one of the pre-made ones (which are still fresh as they make them daily). I also change a few other things to my order most times. And she got it right the first time. Secondly, I noticed she looked at me more than she did at the register while taking my order. She did look at the register, but her visual contact with me was amazing. It was then I realized this dear lady was not only great in customer service but she was very hip with technology as well. She had learned how to work the register and serve her customers well by giving them an overall five star experience in just ordering chicken. This is pretty common with most of the cashiers at Chick-Fil-A in my estimation.

So why are you telling about this experience then? Thanks for asking…

So, I paid for the food with my phone app, and then thanked her. I had to ask her, "Ma 'am, if you don't mind me asking, how long have you been working on the front line here?" She replied smiling, "Oh, just one week now!" I said, "No, I mean how long you have been here in total?" She said with a bigger smile, "just one week, sir!"

She knew where I was going with this inquiry so she kindly took the lead in the conversation and said, "I'll just tell you sir, I love my new job. I am 85 years old, I love technology and I work for fun not because I have to! But, they pay me! I told them in my interview that I would only work if they put me on the register during peak times. Peak times are when the restaurant is busiest. I learned this system after an hour of training on it and I have been on the front from that day. I am having a ball," she exclaimed!

I couldn't believe what I was seeing, experiencing or hearing. She was 85 and outperforming most on the front line that day in how accurately and rapidly she was assisting customers. She was moving twice as fast as most of the other younger cashiers in the restaurant.

She refused to get stuck in the past. Decade after decade after decade, she kept moving!

What about you?

Will you be my childhood neighborhood or the 85 year old lady…?

SEVEN
Move On

As we have jointly walked together through the chapters of this book it has been a pleasure to write every word with you in mind.

This book is for YOU!

Admittedly, I do not know you by name or your reason for reading the book. But, I am so grateful to be a part of your life journey forward.

You and I have traveled a number of roads together in this read. Some straight, some curvy, some narrow, some bumpy, some smooth, some well-lit, some dark, some long, some short, some scenic, some bland, some under construction.

Some of the roads you must finish before you can turn on to a new one. Some roads you need to exit at the very next cloverleaf to get onto the correct path. Other roads you will travel on them again and again in order to learn the way more perfectly.

Just remember, whatever you do, the key is to keep moving.

Don't park. Don't get stuck.

I have prayed that during the time you read this book you will *MOVE ON and refuse to be stuck.*

I am sure you also have a hope or a prayer that the book will help you to *MOVE ON and refuse to be stuck.*

I also know that this is the desire of the Lord for you to *MOVE ON and refuse to be stuck.*

Look at what he says through the Old Testament Prophet, Isaiah.

"But the Lord says, "Do not cling to events of the past or dwell on what happened long ago. Watch for the new thing I am going to do. It is happening already—you can see it now" Isaiah 43:18-19

WOW! Think about these great promises and instructions.

Don't cling to the past

Don't dwell on the things that happened to you

Look for the new thing that HE will do for you

It has already started to happen for you

You can see the difference already

What a list! Hey, I have an idea!

The moment you close this book, why not take the five statements from the Lord through Isaiah, and write them in your journal or wherever you write important notes. Under each line write down observations that clearly allow you to see where you were when you first started to read this book — *your past* — and where you are now — *the difference you see already.*

You are going to be amazed at the small but significant steps you have already taken that are making a BIG difference. Every step matters. So be sure not to minimize your small steps. Fully embrace them for this is how you *MOVE ON`*

And Old Chinese Proverb reminds us…

"It is better to take many small steps in the right directions than to make a great leap forward only to stumble backward"

I have provided twenty-six small steps for you all beginning with the letters in the alphabet.

As you read through my twenty six points may they serve you with encouragement and fortitude. May they be a go-to for strength. May they serve as a gentle reminder, push or even a hug to assure you that you will MOVE ON.

Are you ready? Let's go...

A. Anger and apathy will not control me
B. Bitterness will not define me
C. Crying will help me to become stress-free
D. Doubt will not hinder my faith
E. Emotions will not threaten me
F. Fear will not torment me
G. Grief will not imprison my soul
H. Happiness will replace hate and hurt in me
I. Inspiration will lift my soul up, Up, UP
J. Joy will give me strength
K. Kindness will be my daily attitude
L. Loneliness will not keep me alone
M. Music will make me dance
N. Nonsense will not befriend me
O. Oppression will not depress me
P. Praise will edify me
Q. Quiet times will help me reflect and repair
R. Regret will not leave me feeling defeated
S. Sadness will turn to happiness and healing
T. Trust will be my friend not fear
U. Understanding will guide me
V. Voices in my life will help me and not hinder me
W. Worthlessness... not me. I am valuable
X. Xeroxing the good and shedding the bad stuff
Y. Yelling will not be my first language
Z. Zestful shall be the tenure of my life

You now have a choice of twenty six ways you can keep moving on every day. If one of these does not work for you, makeup your own.

Just

MOVE ON… Refuse to Stay Stuck!

Afterword

By: Mark J. Chironna

The state of being stuck is more common than most of us might care to admit or realize. From a perspective of psychology, to be stuck involves some level of internal resistance, where life gets suspended in a holding pattern of sorts. That holding pattern is always revealed as something that has been tethered emotionally to an issue. Most issues, if not all of them are relational. They involve either our relationship with God, with ourselves, with others, or with creation itself or our purpose in it. As those who are made in the image of God, we are constantly making meaning of what we experience. "What does this mean?" is a question we are either asking consciously or unconsciously whenever we face a challenge, encounter something new, or find ourselves repeating the known past instead of entering the desired-yet-unknown future.

How we see and however we perceive ourselves and what we are experiencing, determines the manner in which we interpret those experiences. Our way of seeing and observing determines our way of making meaning, or interpreting our various definitions of reality. We like predictability because for the most part, while we love the thought of adventure, we are usually quite comfortable with what we know, and quite uncomfortable with what we don't know.

Tolerating uncertainty takes a certain kind of "way of seeing" that has to be acquired. As creatures of habit, we want to know that when we take certain steps based on certain decisions we will obtain predictable results (even when we claim we want what cannot be predicted). We get 'habituated" to certain ways of seeing reality that then become ways of interpreting reality that after enough time make our patterns in life consistent and, "predictable". We like the fact that our memory serves to remind us of what has worked in the past when we have taken specific actions. After all, if it worked in the past, it stands to reason that it will work in the future if we take similar actions. However, sometimes what worked in the past doesn't work in the future and we miss seeing something that might be obvious to others yet is not obvious to us. Now what? We often revert to changing our actions, hoping for a different result.

The sad reality is that we just might find that no matter what new actions we take, we are still repeating something we have no desire to repeat. Something isn't working. Something, whatever that "something" is, is resisting us. As a result, we can't move on, because we are stuck. Since we are relational creatures, related to God, self, others, and purpose in Creation, we look for ways of overcoming the resistance with the help of others. The challenge, however, when we are stuck is that we tend to keep attempting new actions or ask others for the actions they would recommend.

More often than not, we just might find ourselves compiling all sorts of "solutions" that don't work to get us unstuck. What needs to change? The answer is often obvious, yet undiscerned. We need to change the way we see what we are looking at. Unless we change our observations and perceptions, our interpretations (the meaning we make of what we are experiencing) remains the same. No actions we take will bring about the desired freedom from being stuck in issues: emotions, embedded physiological responses to dysfunctional patterns, cycles of inefficient thought that lead to worry and anxiety (and even depression). The one thing we want, getting unstuck, doesn't happen.

We can feel like life is like the game of the Chinese Finger Traps that we used to get at the amusement park. The finger trap wrapped around your index fingers on both ends the woven fabric tube. The moment you put both fingers in the trap and tried to get free, the tighter the woven cylindrical band became. While medically, if you had a fractured finger this could be beneficial for a season, if you simply wanted to free up your hands once again, it could be quite frustrating to say the least. The solution to getting unstuck is to stop tightening up your fingers and pulling, and simply let go and relax. Well, it's the same with getting unstuck from all the dynamics of the unwanted, repeated patterns of the affairs and vicissitudes of life.

How do we get unstuck? We have to change our way of seeing what we are wrestling with, whatever that might be. How do we change our way of seeing what we are wrestling with? We have to become aware of the way we are seeing what we are dealing with, which brings me to my point: I have had a long-standing and fruitful relationship with my dear friend and co-laborer in the Gospel, Walter Boston Jr.

I have always appreciated his wisdom and his wit, and his adept skill at coming alongside people and guiding their footsteps into places of flourishing and well-being. He has a way of sharing the truths of the Gospel that are powerful and practical at the same time. He is one of the most articulate voices I know.

This little book you hold in your hand is your best opportunity right now to get unstuck from whatever life 'finger-traps' you find yourself immobilized by. "Move On: Refuse To Stay Stuck" is going to teach you how to become more aware of what you are dealing with in your stuck state, reinterpret it in light of the truth, change your perception, change your perspective, change your interpretation and the meaning you are making from it all, and move on!

Enjoy the journey as the Man of God, Walter Boston Jr., invites you to a whole new place from which to view your reality. Once that changes, everything else will change and you will indeed "Move On!"

Bishop Mark J. Chironna

Mark Chironna Ministries

Church On The Living Edge

Longwood, Florida

NOTES

CHAPTER ONE

NOTES

CHAPTER TWO

NOTES

CHAPTER THREE

NOTES

CHAPTER FOUR

NOTES

CHAPTER FIVE

NOTES

CHAPTER SIX

NOTES

CHAPTER SEVEN

NOTES

OTHER SPECIAL NOTES